EMPOWERING MINORITY STUDENTS

Jim Cummins

CALIFORNIA ASSOCIATION FOR BILINGUAL EDUCATION
926 J Street, Suite 810
Sacramento, CA 95814

916/447-3986

DEDICATION

This book is dedicated to all teachers who strive to make children's bilingualism part of the solution rather than part of the problem

First edition 1989

Cover design: Carol Gee

SPECIAL RECOGNITION

CABE is honored to have been chosen by Dr. Jim Cummins to publish his book.

Dr. Cummins, of the Modern Language Centre at the Ontario Institute for Studies in Education in Toronto, specializes in bilingual education for minority and majority students. He has published several highly regarded books in this field.

The CABE membership can take pride in their dedication and generous contribution to CABE's work to ensure excellence in education for *all* students. It is because of these accomplishments that the author selected CABE for publication of this important work, which is a critical extension of the bilingual framework.

CABE expresses its appreciation to Dr. Guillermo Lopez and the Bilingual Education Office of the California State Department of Education for their leadership in introducing Dr. Cummins and his work to the field. Through Dr. Lopez' wisdom and foresight, Dr. Cummins' work was developed into a framework which has effectively guided California in its visionary work with language minority students.

CORPORATE SPONSORSHIP

CABE acknowledges Santillana Publishing Company for its generous technical assistance and for the printing of this book. CABE also expresses its appreciation for Santillana's pioneering efforts in meeting the needs of language minority students, and for its many years of continuing support for CABE and Bilingual Education from the very beginning.

TABLE OF CONTENTS

TABLE OF CONTENTS

FOREWORD

During the past ten years I have spent countless hours discussing with educators in both the United States and Canada causes for the educational difficulties of certain groups of minority students and ways of helping these students succeed educationally. This book is the outcome of those discussions. It represents a collaborative effort that draws on the energy, insights, and dedication of many educators.

The theoretical framework elaborated in the book attempts to distill the essential features of the programs that I have seen working for minority students and the characteristics of educators who have made these programs work. Almost invariably, programs that succeed in promoting minority students' academic growth develop in students a strong sense of confidence in who they are and in their ability to learn. They empower students. The educators who have initiated and taught in these programs have had the personal confidence and courage to defend them against reactions ranging from scepticism to overt racism.

The extremely strong opposition to programs that promote bilingual students' linguistic talents and foster a secure sense of identity is not difficult to explain. These programs challenge a division of power and status in the society (i.e. a power structure) that has been established over centuries. In the past, the majority of Hispanic, Black and Native American students have dropped out of school and have occupied the same low-paying and low-status jobs that their parents occupied. Schools historically have reflected the societal power structure by eradicating minority students' language and identity and by attributing their school failure to inherent deficiencies (e.g. genetic inferiority).

During the late sixties and early seventies, policy-makers and educators in both Canada and the United States (and in other western countries) began to take seriously notions of equality and justice that, prior to then, had been honored primarily at a rhetorical level. In Canada, the federal policy of multiculturalism was designed to promote tolerance and equality for all ethnocultural groups and to eradicate racism from societal institutions. In the United States, the *Equality of Educational Opportunity* provisions aimed to counteract discrimination of all types in the educational system.

It would be unrealistic, however, to expect all manifestations of discrimination to disappear overnight since this discrimination has been supported by societal institutions over many generations. Thus, despite the fact that the societal commitment to overcome discrimination is genuine and strong (and vast amounts of money have been committed to this in the United States), there are many forces in the society that operate to preserve traditional power and status divisions. Education (or the lack of it) has always been a major means of reinforcing the social status and economic structures that exist in the society. For example, it was a crime in the United States to teach black slaves to read because literacy, as Paolo Freire has demonstrated so well, is a first step towards liberation.

However, the fact that obvious forms of discrimination can no longer be tolerated by the society, requires that educational programs that continue to disable minority children be disguised as being in children's own best interests. Thus, the eradication of minority students' language and pride is justified as necessary to help them learn English. By the same token, programs that empower minority children must either be ignored or their effects distorted.

Educators who are committed to empowering minority children and their communities have become aware of how these subtle forms of discrimination operate and have consciously challenged the power structure both in their classrooms and schools and in the society at large. They have redefined their roles such that they are no longer willing to reflect the societal power structure; as advocates for children and communities, they are committed to transforming their societies by taking seriously notions such as equality, justice and freedom.

This book attempts to explore some of the ways in which the societal power structure has been, and is being, reflected in the education system. The pattern is very clear historically in most western countries. During the past twenty years, however, changes have occurred, with the result that more minorities have, in Richard Rodriguez' phrase "got inside the door." This means that the conflict and debate between those who wish to preserve the existing power structure and those who wish to transform it have become more intense. In the United States, bilingual education, in particular, is seen as a threat to the existing power structure because it institutionalizes and legitimizes the use of a traditionally stigmatized language at a time when the Hispanic population is growing rapidly. Thus, considerable energy has been expended in debating the extent to which bilingual education is in children's best interests. Chapters 3 and 4 examine some of the psychoeducational evidence related to this question.

In Chapters 5 and 6 a causal model for explaining minority children's school failure is outlined. On the basis of this causal model, an intervention model for reversing this failure is articulated and concrete examples of how these intervention strategies can be implemented are discussed.

Chapter 7 examines the arguments made by academic critics of bilingual education. One is immediately struck by the fact that despite the intense controversy surrounding bilingual programs, relatively few academics or researchers have disputed the research data and their interpretation. The majority of academics who argue against bilingual education virtually ignore the research data and revert to conventional wisdoms about the self-evident validity of English immersion. In other words, their approach is not very different from that of the media.

The final chapter places the educational issues into a broader framework by examining parallels between the operation of dominant-dominated power structures in the domestic and international arenas. The ways in which the dominant group attempts to counteract the "internal threat" of bilingual education and minority group empowerment are very similar to the ways in which powerful countries have attempted to reverse political and social changes in less powerful countries that are perceived as threatening their economic and strategic interests. In both cases, disinformation is used to promote domestic acceptance of continued control by the dominant group, empirical realities that contradict the rhetoric are denied or dismissed with the help of the media, and blatant logical inconsistencies are ignored. The primary example that I discuss of this process operating in the international arena is the Reagan administration's paranoia about the "threat" posed to the most powerful nation in the world by a country as tiny and as economically vulnerable as Nicaragua.

Ironically, the domestic and international spheres are linked insofar as the eradication of the United States' "homegrown" linguistic resources contributes to the creation of a nation of "monolinguistic bumpkins"[1] that is internationally isolated and subject to communication difficulties in dealing with other nations. External "threats" to U.S. security and economic health could be resolved much more effectively by a linguistically-competent nation.

In a fundamental sense, educators who empower minority students by promoting their linguistic talents are also empowering their nation, and to a much greater extent than those who have committed themselves to squandering its human resources.

This book does not attempt to provide a comprehensive overview of of all issues in the education of minority students. Other authors have treated

---

[1]The words are those of former Education Secretary Terrel Bell who served in the early years of the Reagan administration.

many of the issues in more depth (e.g. Hakuta, 1986; Ovando and Collier, 1985). What I have tried to do is to sketch the dimensions of the whole picture in such a way that concrete and realistic directions for change are indicated. Thus, although the effectiveness or otherwise of bilingual education has been the focus of public controversy, bilingual programs represent only one aspect of a much broader change process required to reverse minority students' educational failure. The goals of bilingual education can be achieved only when implemented in conjunction with interactive/experiential approaches to pedagogy and with strong parental involvement. By the same token, interactive/experiential pedagogy and non-condescending forms of parental involvement require acceptance of children's linguistic talents and promotion of pride in their cultural background. The common element in all of these approaches is that, when implemented appropriately, they empower minority students. Thus, bilingual education, in itself, is not the major issue. The issue is the extent to which educators, individually and collectively, are prepared to use their creative energies to devise and implement programs that challenge the racist attitudes and institutions that historically have disempowered minority communities and students.

Although the primary focus of the analysis concerns *language* minority students, I believe that the causal model of school failure and the intervention model are equally relevant to *all* minority students. The pattern of educational failure of black students, and the ways in which discriminatory school programs have been rationalized, are essentially similar to the experience of Hispanic and Native students. The school failure of Hispanic and Native students for whom English is the dominant language (see, for example, Dolson, 1985; National Assessment of Educational Progress, 1983) further illustrates the importance of the broader sociopolitical context which the school has historically reflected.

The book focuses primarily on the United States context. However, the central issue of how the societal power structure is replicated educationally goes beyond any one context. Thus, the theoretical framework and intervention model are, I believe, applicable to other minority education situations, depending on the extent to which the historical patterns and current educational realities are similar. For example, there are clear parallels with respect to goals, justifications and outcomes, in the way western countries (e.g. Australia, Canada, Scandinavian countries, the United States) have treated aboriginal or indigenous peoples for centuries and in the ways in which policy-makers in these countries rationalized cultural genocide as "education." In short, the book is not aimed only at the United States context but rather uses that context as a case study to elucidate more general themes.

FOREWORD

Many people helped in bringing this book to fruition. An initial version was prepared for the Teacher Training Monograph Series of the University of Florida and I am grateful to Clemens Hallman and Sandra Fradd for their encouragement. My thanks also go to Ellen Jeske who created the figures and tables and to John Lasruk who drew the illustrations. I have discussed the ideas presented in the book with many colleagues and students and their input has certainly influenced the work in significant ways. Four anonymous reviewers provided valuable suggestions that I have tried to incorporate. I am grateful also to Hugo Baetens Beardsmore, Norm Gold and Naomi Silverman for feedback and encouragement. Four colleagues and friends, in particular, have provided inspiration and influenced my work over a number of years: Alma Flor Ada, Tove Skutnabb-Kangas, Merrill Swain and Lily Wong Fillmore. Hopefully, these pages reflect not only their ideas but also their spirit of commitment.

I would also like to acknowledge the input of many members of the California Association for Bilingual Education (CABE) both to the ideas in the book and to its ultimate publication. My own education with respect to the schooling of language minority students has come about in no small measure as a result of collaboration with CABE. In particular, I am grateful to Shelly Spiegel-Coleman for her enthusiasm about the book and help in the publication process.

Finally, I would like to share some words that I first heard more than ten years ago that express eloquently and simply what this book is all about. Professor Mary Ashworth of the University of British Columbia, speaking at the Ontario TESL conference, noted the fact that the roots of the term *education* imply drawing out children's potential, making them more than they were; however, when children come to school fluent in their primary language and they leave school essentially monolingual in English, then our schools have negated the meaning of the term *education* because they have made children *less* than they were.

Jim Cummins
December 1988

CHAPTER 1

INTRODUCTION

In the summer of 1981 I taught a course with Lily Wong Fillmore at the University of California at Berkeley on the learning of English by minority students. A topic that was discussed frequently during the course was why some minority groups seemed to fare better than others in schools; in particular, several teachers noted the relatively good performance of some Asian groups compared to the persistent difficulties faced by Hispanic and Black students. I remember examining some computer outputs of the CTBS scores of grade 5 and 6 ESL students in a local school district and being struck by the consistent pattern that emerged: in Science and Math Asian students tended to score in the 70-80 percentile range and around the 50th percentile in the areas of Reading and Language Arts. The Hispanic students, by contrast, tended to perform close to average in Math and Science (40 - 50th percentile range), but few made it above the 25th percentile in Reading and Language areas.

This pattern was repeated across classes and could not easily be explained by social class or length of time in the United States. It also seemed implausible to suppose that Asian students were better language learners or more academically gifted than other groups. Several hypotheses and speculations were offered both by Lily Wong Fillmore and myself and by the teachers to account for the pattern of inter-group differences in academic achievement. It was suggested, for example, that Chinese parents might place more value on educational success than Hispanic parents; this hypothesis however, was not supported by ongoing research being carried out by Lily which showed different socialization patterns in Chinese and Hispanic homes but equally high academic expectations for their children. Some teachers in the course also suggested that many teachers tended to have lower expectations for Hispanic children and this might contribute negatively to their school progress. It was also suggested that Chinese children (for whatever reason) are better test-takers and that standardized tests often overestimate their real understanding of a subject; by the same token, these tests may underestimate the knowledge and skills of Hispanic students.

Needless to say, this issue was not resolved during the course but for me it was an issue that persisted because it raised some fundamental questions not only about language learning and academic development but also about the assumptions underlying current policies and programs for language minority students. For example, if there were such differences in academic outcomes for groups exposed to the same educational programs (and research since the mid-60's had indicated these trends), why were these differences not taken into account in developing policies and in planning programs for minority students?

The usual rationale for bilingual education also seemed to be called into question by the large differences among minority groups; for example, it could hardly be argued convincingly that a home-school language switch inevitably led to academic difficulties when many minority students exposed to this type of language switch or "mismatch," seemed to perform well in school. If a home-school language switch or linguistic mismatch were not the fundamental explanation of Hispanic students' academic difficulties, then what was? It seemed clear that sociocultural factors in addition to linguistic and psychological factors had to be considered. Any overall explanation had to account for the fact that language minority groups from similar socioeconomic backgrounds and exposed to basically similar educational programs showed such different educational outcomes.

If sociocultural factors are crucial, then what are these sociocultural factors and how do they interact with different aspects of the schooling minority children receive? How do sociocultural and psychoeducational factors combine to produce academic failure in minority students? Might different educational policies and programs interact with sociocultural factors to reverse the pattern of school failure? Expressed differently, what did all this mean for the teacher in the classroom, or the program administrator, or the psychologist, all of whom are professionals dedicated to helping minority students succeed academically. Unless they know why students are failing, it is clearly impossible to rationally plan instruction, programs or assessment that would reverse this pattern of school failure.

Thus, the issue of inter-group differences in academic progress seemed to me to go right to the heart of the volatile bilingual education debate. The "quick-exit" transitional bilingual programs that had been implemented and the alternative all-English programs, favored by many policy-makers, each seemed to be based on inadequate assumptions since only linguistic reasons were given for students' academic failure and no consideration was given to the social and political context. None of the current theories of language learning, cognitive styles, or classroom instruction could account for the pattern of school failure experienced by different groups of minority students. By the same token, none of them provided adequate guidance for educators who were trying to help students succeed in school.

I was convinced that until we could account for why certain groups of minority students were experiencing academic difficulties we, as educators, would not be in a position to plan appropriate interventions to reverse these difficulties. It seemed plausible that the mixed success of many compensatory education programs, including bilingual education, was due to the fact that the programs were based on a limited and probably erroneous understanding of why students were experiencing academic problems.

Major Themes

This short book attempts to answer some of these questions. It reviews what we know about language proficiency, language learning, bilingualism, and academic development among minority students and tries to relate these psychoeducational factors to the social and historical context in which schools operate. As indicated above, I believe it is critical to identify the causes of minority students' academic difficulties and I propose a model for understanding why some groups of students fail. This "causal model" leads logically to an "intervention model"; in other words, a framework for considering what types of interventions are required to reverse the pattern of minority students' school failure.

A third type of model can also be distinguished, namely an "implementation model". Certain *types* of interventions may be identified in the intervention model but there may be a variety of specific ways (i.e. programs or strategies) in which this form of intervention might be implemented. Specific intervention strategies are likely to vary from one location to another depending on local conditions (e.g. community and school resources - both human and material). For example, at the level of pedagogy, the intervention model might specify an instructional program that allows for meaningful interaction and active use of both written and oral language by students. This model might be implemented in one school through encouraging creative writing for real audiences by students. A different school with more resources or specific expertise on the part of teachers might add international communication through computers (e.g. between students in the U.S. and Mexico) to the implementation of this intervention model.

The book will give specific examples of concrete ways in which educators can implement the types of interventions suggested. However, it is not a recipe book that provides teacher-proof instructions that can be implemented automatically. The aim is rather to help professional educators and parents develop an understanding of why some minority children experience difficulty in school and also to suggest ways in which educators and parents working collaboratively can help students overcome these difficulties. In other words, I will present a set of principles that are intended to encourage educators of minority students to generate their own strategies for promoting student growth. This generation of adequate programs and instructional strategies can occur only when educators *critically* examine the implicit assumptions regarding bilingualism, community participation, pedagogy and assessment that underlie their own interactions with minority students.

A major emphasis of the book is that the kind of education that minority students experience is very much a consequence of the ways in which teachers and other educators have defined their own roles both within the school and in relation to minority communities. In other words, although there are many aspects of children's schooling that are beyond the control of educators in particular settings (e.g. State regulations, attitudes and support from school board administrators, etc), there are also many aspects that are within their control. For example, classroom teachers convey crucial messages in subtle ways to minority students about the validity (or lack of validity) of their language and cultural identity; they provide (or fail to provide) opportunities for students to express this identity through sharing their experiences with other students and adults by means of active use of written and oral language; in addition, classroom teachers have a choice with respect to the extent to which they collaborate with minority parents as partners in a shared enterprise; specifically, they can either explore with parents ways of promoting children's literacy at home or alternatively, they can ignore any potential contribution parents might make to their children's academic growth.

I argue that these (and other) kinds of interventions become possible only when educators define (either explicitly or implicitly) their role as *empowering* minority students. Students who are empowered by their interactions with educators experience a sense of control over their own lives and they develop the ability, confidence, and motivation to succeed academically. They participate competently in instruction as a result of having developed a confident cultural identity and appropriate strategies for accessing the information or resources they require in order to carry out academic tasks to which they are committed. In other words, through their role of empowering students, individual educators represent a major force in reversing school failure among minority students. It is in the interactions with individual educators that minority students are either empowered, or alternatively, disabled, personally and academically.

However, educators can empower students only if they themselves are empowered; in other words, only if they are secure in their own personal and professional identities and confident that they have the ability and administrative support to help students succeed academically. Increasingly, however, educators are being stripped of the possibility of influencing what and how they teach. Current educational "reforms" are reducing teachers to disempowered transmitters of neutralized content (see

Darling-Hammond, 1985; Giroux and McLaren, 1986). The omnipresent standardized test controls the curriculum and limits the extent to which teachers can risk showing imagination, creativity and initiative in their classrooms. Such "off-task" behaviors are less likely to boost test scores than drilling students in test-related content. Consequently, students, teachers, principals and administrators who have focused on education rather than test scores may appear suspect because they don't have the "hard data" to "prove" that they are doing a good job.

By the same token, critical thinking and questioning of authority by teachers is seldom encouraged by those at higher levels of the educational hierarchy. However, if educators are not themselves critical thinkers who are willing to challenge the system within which they operate, they are unlikely to encourage their students to critically analyze and creatively resolve problems. The reciprocal nature of the empowering process is a theme that runs throughout the book.

I argue that when educators fail to adopt a critical stance in relation to the society and schools in which they participate, they themselves become victimized. They are victims because the educational and societal structure which they have passively accepted is one that historically has disabled, and continues to disable, minority students. The operation of this underlying disabling structure has frustrated well-intentioned educators from achieving their professional goals of helping children succeed academically and personally.

For educators at all levels of the educational hierarchy to achieve their professional goals and become empowered in the process, it is necessary to have a vision of the kinds of students and society we are attempting to develop. There is currently a clear disjunction between the rhetoric contained in many school district policy/philosophy statements and the reality of what is happening increasingly in classrooms. The rhetoric endorses the goal of building on the foundation that students bring to school in order to develop individuals who are critical and creative thinkers, who have a strong sense of self-esteem, and who are confident in their ability both to learn and to participate effectively in a democratic society.

Unfortunately, the reality is that schools continue to promote rote memorization rather than critical thinking and encourage consumption of pre-determined knowledge rather than generation of original ideas; the curriculum has been sanitized such that students rarely have the opportunity to discuss critically or write about issues that directly affect the society they will form. Issues such as racism, environmental pollution, U.S. policy in Central America, genetic engineering, global nuclear destruction, arms control, etc. are regarded as too "sensitive" for fragile and impressionable young minds. Instead, students are fed a neutralized diet of social studies, science, and language arts that is largely irrelevant to the enormous global problems that our generation is creating for our children's generation to resolve.

The same disjunction between rhetoric and reality is evident in the fact that in place of self-esteem and a strong sense of cultural identity, schools have systematically promoted ambivalence and insecurity in minority children by punishing them for speaking their first language (L1) and by devaluing their cultural roots. In addition, despite the rhetoric of equity, schools have also very efficiently reproduced the social structure of our societies such that the vast majority of students whose parents have menial and low-paying jobs leave school educated only to a level where they can occupy the same social niche.

This disjunction between rhetoric and reality should cause all of us, as educators, to critically examine the implicit assumptions that underlie our interactions with minority students. To what extent has the overt racism of the past simply become the covert (well-intentioned) racism of the present? To what extent have interventions such as compensatory education, bilingual education, and other large-scale programs simply added a new veneer to the outward facade of the structure that disables minority students? To what extent does the so-called "educational reform" movement simply reinforce the sanitized curriculum that all children receive, thereby contributing to the educational disabling of minority students? In short, minority students can become empowered only through interactions with educators who have critically examined and, where necessary, challenged the educational (and social) structure within which they operate.

Organization

The second chapter reviews the historical and current political context of the education of minority students in the United States. The issues in the debate are identified and the data on the extent of minority students' school failure are briefly reviewed. Chapters 3 and 4 discuss several psychoeducational principles that are supported by a considerable amount of research and theory. These principles deal with the nature of language proficiency, the effects of bilingualism, the relationship between first (L1) and second (L2) languages, and the determinants of second language acquisition. The fifth chapter discusses the causes of academic failure among minority students and outlines a framework for intervention aimed at reversing this pattern of failure. The implementation of this intervention model is illustrated in Chapter 6 with reference to specific programs and strategies. In Chapter 7 the arguments presented by academic critics of bilingual education are examined in order to assess the extent to which their reading of the research evidence provides an alternative basis for policy with respect to minority students. The conclusion reached is that virtually all of these critics either ignore the research evidence itself or ignore the role of theory in interpreting the research evidence. For the most part, the arguments of academic critics of bilingual education differ very little from those of media commentators in that they substitute an emotional appeal regarding the self-evident validity of English immersion in place of any rational discussion of the research. Finally, in Chapter 8, historical and current policies with respect to domestic minority groups are placed in the context of the power relations between rich and poor nations. It is argued that there is a clear parallel between the formerly overt and currently covert racism that certain domestic minority groups experience and the historical and current exploitation of poor nations by the rich. The academic failure of minority groups in the United States and other countries can be understood as a function of the fact that these groups have had, and continue to a considerable extent to have, the status of internal colonies.

CHAPTER 2

HISTORICAL AND POLITICAL CONTEXT

The Historical Context

Many commentators have objected strenuously to the implementation of bilingual education programs because they appear to run counter to the American tradition of assimilating immigrant groups into the mainstream of society. To these commentators, the increased status that accrues to a language (e.g. Spanish) as a result of being recognized for instructional purposes in schools appears likely to hinder the efficient operation of the melting pot. Not only will individuals who speak that language be rewarded with jobs and other incentives, but children will also be encouraged to retain their language. To opponents of bilingual education the apparent encouragement of ethnic distinctiveness is especially unpalatable at the present time since the rapid growth of the Spanish-speaking population is already posing a threat to the dominance of the Anglo majority in several parts of the country (e.g. Florida, Southern California). A favourite theme of many commentators is that the melting pot worked well for previous generations of immigrants who "made it" without crutches, and Hispanic children could also make it if they tried (Cummins, 1981a).

This attitude shows a profound ignorance of American educational history. The groups that currently tend to experience the most educational difficulty (Black, Hispanic and Native American) were never given the opportunity to "melt" into the American mainstream. Unlike immigrant groups, these three groups have had the status of "internal colonies" in that they have been conquered, subjugated, and regarded as inherently inferior for generations by members of the dominant Anglo group.

In fact, from a historical point of view, the concerns about bilingual education being against American traditions and a potential catalyst for Hispanic separatist tendencies are somewhat ironic in view of the fact that the education of Mexican-Americans in the Southwest was openly dedicated until the late 1960's to *separating* Mexican-American students from the mainstream of American society by means of segregated schooling (conducted exclusively in English). In Texas, for example, the judgement of the court in the United States versus the State of Texas case (1981) documented the "perversive, intentional discrimination throughout most of this century" against Mexican-American students (a charge that was not contested by the State of Texas in the trial) and noted that:

"the long history of prejudice and deprivation remains a significant obstacle to equal educational opportunity for these children. The deep sense of inferiority, cultural isolation, and acceptance of failure, instilled in a people by generations of subjugation, cannot be eradicated merely by integrating the schools and repealing the 'no Spanish' statutes" (1981, p. 14).

Noel Epstein (1977), although a critic of bilingual education policy, has also noted "the widespread discrimination and humiliation that have often been severely inflicted against such students" (p. 55). He goes on to report that

"As late as 1970, Charles E. Silberman reported, 'In a South Texas school, children are forced to kneel in the playground and beg forgiveness if they are caught talking to each other in Spanish; some teachers require students using the forbidden language to kneel before the entire class.' In the early 1970's, the U.S. Civil Rights Commission reported comments from students who said that getting caught speaking Spanish meant that they were fined, forced to stand on a special black square or made to write 'I must not speak Spanish.' This may help explain why Hispanic Americans speak of the melting pot today in harsh terms which other Americans might not recognise" (p. 55).

This Hispanic view of the melting pot is eloquently expressed in an essay by Isidro Lucas (1981) entitled "Bilingual Education and the Melting Pot: Getting Burned." He argues that

"There is in America a profound, underground culture, that of the *unmeltable* populations. Blacks have proven unmeltable over the years. The only place allowed them near the melting pot was underneath it. Getting burned. Hispanics were also left out of the melting pot. Spanish has been historically preserved more among them than other languages in non-English-speaking populations. It was a shelter, a defense. The days when Texas establishments would post a sign at the door, 'No niggers, no dogs, no Mexicans' are not too far in the past" (p. 21-22).

Segregated/inferior schooling was usually rationalized on the grounds that it was necessary in order to provide effective remedial instruction in English to students who were "language handicapped" (Schlossman, 1983). However, in the Southwest, Hispanic children were generally assigned to segregated schools purely on the basis of surname when in fact many knew more English than Spanish since English had been the dominant home language for generations (Sanchez, 1943). George Sanchez, in many articles, pointed to the racism that was rationalized by

"thinly veiled [pedagogical] excuses which do not conform with either the science of education or the facts in the case. Judging from current practice, these pseudo-pedagogical reasons call for short school terms, ramshackle school buildings, poorly paid and untrained teachers, and all varieties of prejudicial discrimination" (1943, p. 16; quoted in Schlossman, 1983, p. 893).

The discrimination against dominated minority children may persist in more subtle ways even in non-segregated classrooms. For example, a large-scale study conducted by the U.S. Commission on Civil Rights (1973) reported that majority students were praised or encouraged 36% more often than Mexican-American students and their classroom contributions were used or built upon 40% more frequently than those of Mexican-American students. In all positive categories the majority students experienced more interaction whereas the minority students experienced more interaction only with respect to criticism and being given directions. This discriminatory interaction usually operates in an unconscious way and appears to be a consequence of the diminished expectations that teachers have for students perceived as low achievers (Brophy and Good, 1974).

In short, the discrimination that exists against certain minority groups in the wider society has often been reproduced (inadvertantly in most cases) in the interactions children experience in school. The overt racism has become covert, the violence against minority children has shifted from physical to psychological.

For Native American children, education usually involved segregation not only from the mainstream culture but also from their own families. As described by Platero for Navajo students, the results have frequently been devastating:

"For nearly a hundred years the policy of the United States government was to acculturate the Navajo, so that the Navajo could be assimilated into the White society. To effect this assimilation Navajo children were taken from the shelter of the family and sent to boarding school. Almost every child who entered the boarding school spoke only Navajo, and most of the people employed at the boarding schools spoke only English.

> When a Navajo child spoke the language of his family at school, he was punished. ... Kee was sent to boarding school as a child where - as was the practice - he was punished for speaking Navajo. Since he was only allowed to return home during Christmas and summer, he lost contact with his family. Kee withdrew both from the White and Navajo worlds as he grew older, because he could not comfortably communicate in either language. ... By the time he was 16, Kee was an alcoholic, uneducated and despondent - without identity. Kee's story is more the rule than the exception (Platero, 1975, p. 57-58).[1]

In fact, eradication of identity was an explicit goal of most residential and missionary schools for Indian students in both the United States and Canada. As expressed more than one hundred years ago by the General Secretary of the Methodist Church of Canada, removal of children from the influence of their homes (for at least five years) was a necessary condition for both salvation and civilization:

> "Experience convinces us that the only way in which the Indians of the Country can be permanently elevated and thoroughly civilized, is by removing the children from the surroundings of Indian home life, and keeping them separate long enough to form those habits of order, industry, and systematic effort, which they will never learn at home. ... The return of children to their houses, even temporarily, has a bad effect, while their permanent removal [back home] after one or two years residence results in the loss of all that they have gained" (letter dated April 2, 1886, from A. Sutherland, General Secretary of the Methodist Church of Canada, Missionary Department to Laurence Vankoughnet, Deputy Superintendent of Indian Affairs. Quoted in Tschantz, 1980, p. 7).

Tschantz goes on to document the extreme violence used in these schools to dissuade children from using their mother tongue, the key to their identity.

> "Dolphus Shae's testimony to the Berger Inquiry (1977:90) of his experiences at the Aklavik Residential School describes not only the terrifying experiences which he and many other children endured, but also the resentment which lasted all his life: 'Before

---

[1]See Skutnabb-Kangas, 1984, for a detailed discussion of violence and minority education.

I went to school the only English I knew was 'hello' and when we got there we were told that if we spoke Indian they would whip us until our hands were blue on both sides. And also we were told that the Indian religion was superstitious and pagan. It made you feel inferior to whites ... We all felt lost and wanted to go home ... Today I think back on the hostel life and I feel furious'" (Tschantz, 1980, p. 10).

Tschantz notes that it is hardly surprising that even as late as 1972, 97% of all Indian students in Canada never graduated from high school. Yet it was only in the 1970's that the Canadian government began to wonder if these figures might be partially attributable to the "education" inflicted on children rather than to their inherent inferiorities.

In both the United States and Canada (and most other countries) the school failure of minority students under conditions of identity eradication through physical and psychological violence was seldom attributed to deficient schooling (except by "radicals" such as George Sanchez); rather, the blame was attributed either to inherent inferiorities of the particular group (e.g. genetic deficiency) or to factors such as bilingualism or "language handicap" (see Hakuta, 1986).

In the case of immigrant minorities, schooling was generally not segregated but the same overt goals (acculturation to the dominant culture) and methods (punishment for speaking the home language) were used. Contrary to popular belief, many first generation immigrant children experienced considerable difficulty in school. Cohen (1970) sums up the findings of a comprehensive review of the educational achievement of immigrant students in the early part of this century as follows:

"the evidence ... suggests that in the first generation, at least, children from many immigrant groups did not have an easy time in school. Pupils from these groups were more likely to be retarded than their native white schoolmates, more likely to make low scores on IQ tests, and they seem to have been a good deal less likely to remain in high school" (1970, p. 24).

Many of these first generation immigrants may have become successful economically since much less education was required for economic and social advancement at the beginning of this century than is the case at the present time.

For the children of these immigrants, there was considerable variability across groups in academic performance; specifically,

"Children whose parents emigrated from England, Scotland, Wales, Germany, and Scandinavia seem to have generally performed about as well in school as native whites. ... The children of Jewish immigrants typically achieved at or above the average for native whites. It was central and southern European non-Jewish immigrants - and to a lesser extent, the Irish - who experienced really serious difficulty in school" (Cohen, p. 24).

Cohen suggests that the ethnic differences in school performance may arise from cultural/motivational factors and the degree of urbanization of the different groups.

It is clear from these data that a complex array of variables determines minority children's academic achievement and that the argument that previous generations of immigrants made it "without the crutch of bilingual education" is seriously oversimplified. However, the data also show that the usual rationale for bilingual education similarly fails to account for the observed pattern. The usual rationale for bilingual programs is that children cannot learn in a language they do not understand and therefore, if there is a home-school "linguistic mismatch," academic retardation will almost invariably result. The historical data show that Scandinavian and German children peformed well despite a mismatch between the language of the home and the language of the school whereas Irish children instructed in their native language (English, for the most part) experienced difficulty.

Research conducted between 1920 and 1960 tended to report that bilingual children performed at considerably lower levels on a variety of cognitive and academic tasks and many also experienced emotional difficulties. Some researchers went so far as to claim that bilingualism led to schizophrenic tendencies and that bilinguals were morally untrustworthy! (See Vildomec, 1963 for a review of these studies). Essentially bilingualism (or some other deficiency within the child) became the scapegoat which "explained" the poor school performance of minority children. Research showing that bilingual children performed lower on verbal IQ tests than monolingual children was interpreted to mean that there is only so much space or capacity available in our brains for language; therefore, if we divide that space between two languages, neither language will develop properly and intellectual confusion will result. The school treatment was taken for granted and not subjected to scrutiny as a possible contributor to minority children's educational difficulties. This pattern of "Blaming the Victim" first described by Ryan (1972) with respect to Black children's education, is outlined in Table 2-1.

In summary, the preceding discussion emphasizes the critical role that

Table 2-1

Blaming the Victim in the Education of Minority Students

A. **OVERT AIM**   **COVERT AIM**

Teach English to minority children   Anglicize minority children because
in order to create a harmonious   linguistic and cultural diversity are
society with equal opportunity for   seen as a threat to social cohesion.
all.

B. **METHOD**   **JUSTIFICATION**

Punish children for using L1 in   1. L1 should be eradicated because
schools and encourage them to   it will interfere with the learning
reject their own culture and language   of English;
in order to identify with majority   2. Identification with L1 culture
English group.   will reduce child's ability to
                                                identify with English-speaking
                                                culture.

C. **RESULTS**   **"SCIENTIFIC" EXPLANATIONS**

1. Shame in L1 language and culture.   1. Bilingualism causes confusion in
                                                thinking, emotional insecurity
                                                and school failure.
2. Replacement of L1 by L2.   2. Minority group children are
                                                "culturally deprived" (almost
                                                by definition since they are not
                                                Anglos).
3. School failure among many   3. Some minority language groups
   children.   are genetically inferior (common
                                                theory in 1920's recently revived
                                                by Lloyd Dunn (1986)).

D. **OUTCOMES**

1. The educational disablement of minority children under these conditions
   only serves to reinforce the myth of minority group inferiority.

2. Even more intense efforts by the school to eradicate the "deficiencies"
   inherent in minority children (i.e. their language and culture).

the social context in general, and in particular, the power relations between ethnic groups, play in determining minority children's language learning and academic achievement. The major points are as follows:

- the minority groups that tend to experience the most severe academic disadvantage have been in a dominated relationship to the Anglo majority for centuries and have never been given the opportunity to assimilate into the American mainstream; on the contrary, they were subjected over generations to segregated and inferior schooling, they were punished for speaking their home language in school, and their pride in their cultural identity was systematically eradicated;

- the educational treatment that these minority children received and the attitudes of educators have tended to reflect the treatment and attitudes that their communities experienced in the wider society; both children and adults have been prevented from full participation and advancement in mainstream societal institutions (e.g. schools, the job market, etc) through segregation and discrimination;

- although early generations of *immigrant* children did tend to experience academic difficulties, they were not discriminated against nor segregated educationally to the same extent as the dominated minorities; thus, an inferior self-image was not internalized by the group and later generations assimilated to the mainstream society and tended to succeed academically;

- school failure on the part of minority students was generally attributed to some inherent deficiency within the child, either genetic or experiential (e.g. cultural deprivation, bilingual confusion, etc); this focus on inherent deficiencies of the minority child served to deflect attention away from the educational treatment that children were receiving;

The Current Political Context: Sociopolitical Concerns and Psychoeducational Rationalizations

Although, as discussed in the previous section, the United States has a history of overt racism against certain minority groups, it is virtually unique among western nations in the extent to which this discrimination has been acknowledged and resources committed to reversing its effects. Various types of compensatory education programs were implemented in the sixties in order to combat the low achievement and high drop-out rates among Black and other minority groups; bilingual education programs followed in the late sixties and seventies in response to the documented school failure of certain groups of linguistic minorities; non-discriminatory testing of minorities was mandated by court decisions in the early seventies and by the federal special education legislation (Public Law [PL] 94-142) which came into effect in 1975; these changes were prompted by data showing massive over-representation of Black and Hispanic children in classes for the mentally retarded (Mercer, 1973).[2]

The legitimacy of this government concern for educational equity appears to be acknowledged by the majority of media commentators, although there is certainly disagreement on the appropriate ways of promoting equality of educational opportunity. A survey of press comment on the education of minority students (Cummins 1981a) showed general agreement that government (at either federal, state or local levels) had a responsibility to discover and implement the educational approaches that would be most effective in reversing inequality.

This task of discovering effective educational programs has proved more difficult than anticipated.   Initially, as Troike (1978) has observed, bilingual education was instituted in the late sixties on the basis of what appeared to be a self-evident rationale, namely that "the best medium for teaching a child is his or her mother tongue," but with relatively little hard evidence to back up this rationale.   The reaction of many press commentators in the initial years of this experiment was one of "wait-and-see"; they didn't particularly like the idea but were willing to give it a chance to prove its potential for reducing educational inequities. Some were concerned, however, that bilingual education might have the opposite effect, namely of preventing Spanish-speaking students from entering the mainstream of English-speaking America, and also that it might give rise to the divisiveness that appeared to be associated with bilingualism in Canada. However, in general, this first phase (1967-1976) of the modern bilingual education debate was marked by a tolerance for the educational potential of bilingual education and, although doubts were certainly raised, its rationale was not disputed in any sustained or systematic way.

---

[2]By contrast with the American concern for educational equity, Canadian educational regulations and provisions reveal little overt concern for such issues (although many individual school boards are very much concerned) and relatively little research has been conducted on issues such as the achievement of different minority groups or non-discriminatory assessment. For example, in Ontario, the Special Education legislation (Bill 82) was modelled after PL94-142 in most respects but unlike PL94-142 no provisions were made for promoting non-discriminatory assessment of minority students (see Cummins, 1984).

An early expression of these views appeared in the Christian Science Monitor (Nov. 13, 1967). The editorial noted that several senators were drafting measures for bilingual education because they were concerned, "and very rightly so," about the educational lag among Spanish-speaking children. However, it went on to wonder

> "whether such an official recognition of Spanish might not actually worsen the situation rather than improve it. Might it not tend to fasten even more strongly upon children the disadvantage of being Spanish-speaking in an overwhelmingly English-speaking land?"

Since the mid-seventies the bilingual education debate has become considerably more volatile and the sociopolitical concerns of many commentators have been backed up by psychoeducational arguments against bilingual education and in favor of all-English "immersion" programs. The linguistic mismatch hypothesis, as expressed in the argument that "children can't learn in a language they don't understand," is no longer regarded as self-evident in view of the fact that findings from French immersion programs in Canada show that English-background children who were taught initially through French in order to develop fluent bilingual skills did not suffer academically as a result of this home-school language shift (see Swain & Lapkin, 1982; Cummins & Swain, 1986). To many commentators in the United States, these results suggested that English immersion programs were a plausible educational alternative to bilingual programs.[3] Furthermore, immersion programs appeared to avoid the potential divisiveness associated with the recognition and institutionalization of Spanish.

The current opposition to bilingual programs is well summed up in the following three quotations which vividly outline the concerns of many Americans about the increasing penetration of Spanish into mainstream institutions such as the educational system:

> "Bilingual education is an idea that appeals to teachers of Spanish and other tongues, but also to those who never did think that another idea, the United States of America, was a

---

[3]As documented in Chapters 4 and 7, most American commentators who use the Canadian French immersion programs to argue for "English immersion" for minority students fail to realize that French immersion programs are fully *bilingual* in that they are taught by bilingual teachers, the goal is bilingualism and biliteracy, and children's L1 is strongly promoted after the initial grades so that about half the instruction is through L1 in grades 4-6.

particularly good one to begin with, and that the sooner it is restored to its component 'ethnic' parts the better off we shall all be. Such people have been welcomed with open arms into the upper reaches of the federal government in recent years, giving rise to the suspicion of a death wish" (Bethell, 1979, p. 30).

President Reagan also joined the fray in early March 1981, arguing that:

"It is absolutely wrong and against American concepts to have a bilingual education program that is now openly, admittedly dedicated to preserving students' native language and never getting them adequate in English so they can go out into the job market and participate." (Democrat-Chronicle, Rochester, March 3, 1981, p. 2A)

The incompatibility that is implied in President Reagan's remark between preserving the native languages of minority students and the learning of English is a theme that occurs frequently in the opposition to bilingual programs. This assumed incompatibility is made explicit in the following excerpt from a New York Times editorial (October 10, 1981):

"The Department of Education is analyzing new evidence that expensive bilingual education programs don't work ... Teaching non-English speaking children in their native language during much of their school day constructs a roadblock on their journey into English. A language is best learned through immersion in it, particularly by children ... Neither society nor its children will be well served if bilingualism continues to be used to keep thousands of children from quickly learning the one language needed to succeed in America."

The general line of argument against bilingual education is clear: such programs are a threat to national unity and furthermore they are ineffective in teaching English to minority students since the primary language, rather than English, is used for a considerable amount of instruction in the early grades. The bilingual approach appears to imply a counter-intuitive "less equals more" rationale in which *less* English instruction is assumed to lead to *more* English achievement. It appears more logical to many opponents of bilingual education to argue that if children are deficient in English then they need instruction in English, not their native language (L1). School failure is caused by *insufficient exposure* to English (at home) and it makes no sense to further dilute the amount of English to which minority students are exposed by instructing them through their L1 at school. Unless such students are immersed in English at school, they will not learn English and consequently will be prevented from participating in the mainstream of American society.

This line of argument was continued by former Secretary of Education William J. Bennett who, in the fall of 1985, described bilingual education as "a failed path" and emphasized the need to provide flexibility to local school districts to decide which instructional approach to follow. As reported in FORUM, the Newsletter of the National Clearinghouse for Bilingual Education:

> "Bennett stressed that learning English is the key to equal educational opportunity and is the unifying bond for the diverse population of the United States. Proficiency in English should thus be the primary objective of special instructional programs for LEP [limited-English-proficient] students, the secretary declared. According to Bennett, federal policy has lost sight of this goal by its emphasis on bilingual education as a means to enhance the students' knowledge of their native language and culture ... The secretary cited research studies, the below-average performance of Hispanics, and the high Hispanic dropout rate as indications that bilingual education programs have not been effective and that federal policy needs adjustment" (Volume 8, number 5, p. 1, October/November 1985).

Two general issues can be raised with respect to the psychoeducational arguments for and against bilingual education. First, what underlying assumptions are implied by these arguments and to what extent are these assumptions valid in light of the research evidence? Second, to the extent that the assumptions are not valid, what sociopolitical function do they serve? In other words, what policies and programs do they legitimize and to what extent do minority students benefit or suffer as a result of these policies and programs?

The arguments about the educational validity of bilingual education embody a variety of assumptions that *can* be tested against the available research evidence. For example, to what extent does research support the "linguistic mismatch" hypothesis that children exposed to a home-school language switch will suffer academic retardation? At the other pole of the debate, is it true that more exposure to English at school increases English academic achievement or does less English instruction lead to more English achievement, as implied by the bilingual education rationale? Is bilingualism an educational disadvantage or might it be a positive force in children's development under some conditions? Is there a positive or a negative relationship between children's L1 and L2 academic skills?

At a more basic level, many commentators on both sides of the issue suggest that lack of English proficiency is the major cause of children's academic disadvantage - is there any evidence for this assumption? It is also relevant to ask what exactly is meant by "English proficiency"? Specifically, how are academic skills in English related to the acquisition of English conversational skills? Clarification of these issues is important in order to answer the central question regarding the most effective methods of promoting English and overall academic development.

Finally, the research evidence regarding the impact both of the sociopolitical context and the instructional treatment in determining minority children's academic development can be examined. The review of the historical context of minority students' education earlier in this chapter suggested that social variables related to inter-group power relations played a major role in determining minority students' academic progress. If so, why have these variables not been taken into account in the policy debate? What is the relationship between sociopolitical and psychoeducational factors in determining student outcomes?

These issues are discussed in the following chapters. The research on most of these issues is sufficiently clear to show that the major psychoeducational arguments against bilingual education are spurious. In fact, massive amounts of research evidence refute the argument that insufficient exposure to English is a major cause of minority students' academic failure. Given the overwhelming evidence against the insufficient exposure assumption, it is legitimate to ask what sociopolitical function such arguments serve. It will be argued that the sociopolitical function of such arguments is very similar to the sociopolitical function of previous arguments used to legitimize sink-or-swim (submersion) programs for minorities. The argument that bilingualism caused "language handicaps" legitimized eradicating minority children's L1 and making them ashamed of their cultural identity. In the same way, current arguments promoting maximum exposure to English serve to emasculate bilingual programs such that relatively ineffective "quick-exit" programs are implemented rather than the considerably more effective programs aimed at promoting biliteracy. In both cases, a patently inferior form of education has been rationalized as being for children's own good and necessary "in order to enable them to learn English."

CHAPTER 3

THE TWO FACES OF LANGUAGE PROFICIENCY

The rationale for bilingual education in the United States as it is understood by most policy makers and practitioners can be stated as follows:

> Lack of English proficiency is the major reason for language minority students' academic failure. Bilingual education is intended to ensure that students do not fall behind in subject matter content while they are learning English, as they would likely do in an all-English program. However, when students have become proficient in English, they can be exited to an all-English program, since limited English proficiency will no longer impede their academic progress.

As pointed out in the previous chapter, there are serious problems with this rationale for bilingual education, despite its intuitive appeal. In the first place, it ignores the sociohistorical determinants of minority students' school failure. Secondly, the question of what exactly constitutes proficiency in English is left vague, despite its central importance to the entire rationale. The purpose of this chapter is to examine what is meant by the notion of "language proficiency" and how minority students' increasing proficiency in conversational English relates to their academic progress.

There are two major misconceptions regarding the nature of language proficiency that have been (and still are) prevalent among educators. These misconceptions have important *practical* implications for the way educators interact with language minority students. Both involve a confusion between the surface or conversational aspects of children's language and deeper aspects of proficiency that are more closely related to children's conceptual and academic development. The first misconception entails identifying children's control over the surface structures of standard English with their ability to think logically. Children who speak a non-standard variety of English (or their L1) are frequently thought to be handicapped educationally and less capable of logical thinking. This assumption derives from the fact that children's language is viewed as inherently deficient as a tool for expressing logical relations.

The second misconception is in many respects the converse of the first. In this case, children's good control over the surface features of English (i.e. their ability to converse adequately in English) is taken as an indication that all aspects of their "English proficiency" have been mastered to the same extent as native speakers of the language. In other words, conversational skills are interpreted as a valid index of overall proficiency in the language. In the case of both of these misconceptions, a close relationship is assumed between the two faces of language proficiency, the conversational and the academic.

Surface Structure Deviations and Academic Progress

In many of the compensatory education programs of the 1960's, language proficiency was identified with control over the surface structures of standard English. Knowledge of standard English, in turn, was viewed as a prerequisite for both logical thinking and educational progress. As summarized by Labov (1970, 1973) differences in the grammatical forms of English used by children from high and low social class groups and by children from different ethnic groups were often equated with differences in children's capacity for logical analysis. It was assumed that children's low scores on (culturally-biased) IQ tests were *caused* by their "deficient" competence in standard English. Then attempts were made to teach children to think logically by requiring them to mimic certain formal speech patterns used by middle-class teachers. The classical statement of these views is that the "language of culturally deprived children ... is not merely an underdeveloped version of standard English, but is a basically non-logical mode of expressive behavior" (Bereiter, Engelmann, Osborn and Reidford, 1966, p. 113). Black students were thought to fail in school because they were not only "culturally deprived" but also "linguistically deprived." These assumptions led to remedial programs such as DISTAR (Englemann and Osborn, 1976) which attempt to develop academic and cognitive skills in "culturally deprived" children by drilling them in rules and structures.

Labov (1970, 1973) points out that this approach "diverts attention from real defects in our educational system to imaginary defects of the child" (1973, p. 22). Furthermore, it rests on extremely naive assumptions about the relationship between linguistic varieties and educational success. Through detailed sociolinguistic analyses of the speech of black adolescents, Labov showed that the logic of nonstandard English cannot be distinguished from the logic of standard English. When assessed in naturalistic situations outside the school context (rather than in a contrived testing situation) black children's speech incorporated conceptual operations and logic at least as complex as that found in typical middle-class speech. Labov attributes the fact that inner-city black children often tend not to manifest their conceptual abilities in school to the negative influence of teachers' expectations. Because teachers tend to equate nonstandard dialect with deficient academic ability, they tend to have low academic expectations for black children and these expectations become self-fulfilling.

Another version of this approach to "language proficiency" is to regard code-switching as an indication of inadequate proficiency in one or both languages. Clearly, children's control of one or both of their languages can vary but code-switching is largely determined by social relations among users of the languages rather than by proficiency in the languages. In itself, code-switching carries no implications with regard to either overall language proficiency or academic achievement. Code-switching, in fact, can be a powerful way of conveying nuances of meaning and emphasizing certain points (Valdes-Fallis, 1978).

A recent example of how persistent some of these linguistic prejudices are among academics comes from a monograph on Hispanic children written by Lloyd Dunn (1987), the primary author of the Peabody Picture Vocabulary Test (PPVT). In expressing his concerns that bilingual education could result in "at least the partial disintegration of the United States of America" (p. 66-67), Dunn argues that Latino children and adults "speak inferior Spanish" and that "Latin pupils on the U.S. mainland, as a group, are inadequate bilinguals. They simply don't understand either English or Spanish well enough to function adequately in school" (p. 49). He goes on to argue that this is due to the fact that these children "do not have the scholastic aptitude or linguistic ability to master two languages well, or to handle switching from one to the other, at school, as the language of instruction" (p. 71). He attributes the causes of this lower scholastic ability of Latino students about equally to environmental factors and "to genes that influence scholastic aptitude" (p. 64).[1] Although the role of schools in contributing to children's academic development is acknowledged, it is largely dismissed on the grounds that "teachers are not miracle workers" (p. 65) and "Hispanic pupils and their parents have also failed the schools and society, because they have not been motivated and

---

[1]Dunn's "evidence" for genetic inferiority is based on the fact that "most Mexican immigrants to the U.S. are brown-skinned people, a mix of American Indian and Spanish blood, while many Puerto Ricans are dark-skinned, a mix of Spanish, black, and some Indian. Blacks and American Indians have repeatedly scored about 15 IQ points behind Anglos and Orientals on individual tests of intelligence" (p. 64). He concludes on the basis of arguments presented by Jensen (1980) and Clarizio (1982) that psychometric tests are not biased against minority children and therefore that those who attribute the IQ test differential to test bias are manifesting "largely an emotional and irrational defense reaction" (p. 62). I find it curious that Dunn makes no reference to the chapter in my book (Cummins, 1984) which discusses in detail the many fallacies in Clarizio's and Jensen's position despite the fact that he cites my book positively (!) numerous times in his monograph.

dedicated enough to make the system work for them" (p. 78). It is not difficult to discern the familiar pattern of "blaming the victim" outlined in Table 2-1.

However, misconceptions about language varieties and their relation to educational progress are not confined only to uninformed academics and policy-makers. Minority educators are equally subject to prejudices regarding the value of different linguistic varieties. In fact, despite the fact that Labov's analysis is universally accepted by linguists and sociolinguists, it is still disturbingly common to find administrators and teachers in bilingual programs disparaging the variety of children's primary language (L1) that they bring to school and attempting to teach the standard variety through decontextualized drills. In some cases this is rationalized on the grounds that children need to know the standard form before they can learn to read in L1; in other cases there is a refusal to tolerate the use of an "inferior" form of the language in educational contexts. Thus, misconceptions regarding language varieties exist both in mainstream and bilingual classrooms.

This tendency can be illustrated by an interchange at a workshop I gave for heritage language teachers in Canada.[2] A participant raised the issue of how to deal with children's nonstandard uses in the classroom. Another teacher immediately raised his hand to share his way of helping children learn the standard form of the language (in this case Italian). He suggested that when children use a nonstandard form in the classroom, the teacher should immediately stop the child and give her the "correct" term or expression. Another participant then asked what he would do if the child said that the nonstandard form was what her parents used. The teacher's response was that the teacher should tell the child that her parents were using the wrong word and that she should go home and tell her parents what the "correct" word was.

It is clear that what is being communicated to the child in this case is that her parents not only have problems in English but that they can't even speak their first language properly. The effect is likely to be to reduce children's pride in their own cultural background and adversely affect their esteem for their own parents. An alternative way of dealing with the same issue was suggested by a teacher of Italian at a different workshop. She suggested that when a nonstandard word comes up in class the teacher can go around the class to see what other words (in different

---

[2]"Heritage languages" is the term used in Canada to refer to minority languages other than French (an official language) and the languages of the aboriginal peoples of Canada [Indian and Inuit or Eskimo].

dialects) children have for this object or idea. Her experience was that children soon realized the need for the standard form of the language in order to facilitate communication between different groups whose native dialects are different. Children also realize that the nonstandard varieties are appropriate and valid within the contexts in which they are typically used and that there is no need to replace the nonstandard form with the standard. The teacher's orientation should be to add the standard form to the child's linguistic repertoire while encouraging continued use of the nonstandard forms in contexts to which they are appropriate.

In summary, there is no basis for attributing either deficient linguistic or cognitive ability to minority children because they use a nonstandard form of either their L1 or English. Children will usually have (or soon develop) receptive knowledge of the standard form of the language and as they continue to interact with speakers of the standard language (e.g. the teacher) they will gradually develop the ability to produce and write the standard form. Provision by the teacher of explicit information about conventions of the standard language (e.g. spelling, grammar) is appropriate and can be useful in the context of tasks to which students are committed. When students want the final product to conform to these conventions, they will be motivated to acquire these conventions. As outlined in Chapter 6, process writing procedures whereby students revise drafts of written work with input from the teacher and other students represent a good example of the kinds of teacher input that are effective in developing students' knowledge of standard forms of the language. However, explicit teaching of the standard form outside of a meaningful communicative context is unlikely to be effective and constant correction of students' oral language may damage their self-esteem.

How Long Does it Take Minority Students to Acquire English?

A considerable amount of research from both Europe and North America suggests that minority students frequently develop fluent surface or conversational skills in the school language but their academic skills continue to lag behind grade norms (Cummins, 1984; Skutnabb-Kangas and Toukomaa, 1976). It is important for educators to be aware of this research since failure to take account of the distinction between conversational and academic language skills can result in discriminatory testing of minority students and premature exit from bilingual programs into all-English programs. Specifically, the presence of adequate surface structure leads teachers and psychologists to eliminate "limited English proficiency" as an explanation for children's academic difficulty. The result is that minority children's low academic performance is attributed to deficient cognitive abilities (e.g. "learning disabilities," educable mental retardation) or to lack of motivation to succeed academically.

Some concrete examples will help illustrate how this process operates. These examples are taken from a Canadian study in which the teacher referral forms and psychological assessments of more than 400 language minority students were analyzed (Cummins, 1984). Throughout the teacher's referral forms and psychologists' assessment reports there are references to the fact that children's English communicative skills are considerably better developed than their academic language skills (e.g. reading achievement). For example:

PS (094):   referred for reading and arithmetic difficulties in grade 2; teacher commented that "since PS attended grade 1 in Italy, I think his main problem is language, although he understands and speaks English quite well."

DM (105):   Arrived from Portugal at age 10 and was placed in a grade 2 class; three years later, in grade 5, her teacher commented that "her oral answering and comprehension is so much better than her written work that we feel a severe learning problem is involved, not just her non-English background."

GG (184):   Although he had been in Canada for less than a year, in November of the grade 1 year the teacher commented that "he speaks Italian fluently and English as well." However, she also referred him for psychological assessment "because he is having a great deal of difficulty with the grade 1 program" and she wondered if he had "specific learning disabilities or if he is just a very long way behind children in his age group."

These examples illustrate the influence of the environment in developing English conversational skills. In many instances in this study language minority students were considered to have sufficient English proficiency to take a verbal IQ test within about a year of arrival in Canada. Similarly, in the United States, language minority students are often considered to have developed sufficient English proficiency to cope with the demands of an all-English classroom after a relatively short amount of time in a bilingual program (in some cases as little as six months).

Recent research suggests that very different time periods are required for minority students to achieve peer-appropriate levels in conversational skills in the second language as compared to academic skills. Specifically, conversational skills often approach native-like levels within about two years of exposure to English whereas a period of five years or more may be required for minority students to achieve as well as native speakers in academic aspects of language proficiency (Collier, 1987; Collier & Thomas, 1988; Cummins, 1981c, 1984; Wong Fillmore, 1983). Academic language proficiency refers to both reading and writing abilities and to content areas where students are required to use their language abilities for learning (e.g. science, social studies, etc).

The pattern is well-illustrated in Collier's studies. These involved more than 2,000 limited-English-proficient students and were carried out in an affluent suburban school district where all instruction was through English. She reported that it took a minimum of 4 to 9 years for these students to attain grade norms in different aspects of English academic skills. It is noteworthy that these figures represent the time period required for the *most advantaged* limited-English-proficient students to perform as well as their native English-speaking peers and a longer time period can be expected for less advantaged students.

The relatively long period of time required for language minority students to attain grade norms in academic aspects of English can be attributed to the fact that native English speakers continue to make significant progress in English academic skills (e.g. vocabulary knowledge, reading and writing skills, etc) year after year. They do not stand still waiting for the minority student to catch up. In conversational skills, on the other hand, after the first six years of life, changes tend to be more subtle.

In addition, in face-to-face conversation the meaning is supported by a range of contextual cues (e.g. the concrete situation, gestures, intonation, facial expression, etc) whereas this is seldom the case for academic uses of language (e.g. reading a text). Typical everyday conversational interactions can be characterized as context-embedded and cognitively-undemanding while academic tasks tend to become increasingly context-reduced and cognitively-demanding as students advance through the grades. The approximate time periods involved in developing peer-appropriate conversational and academic communicative proficiency are outlined in Figure 3-1.

The practical implications of this distinction can be seen in the fact that educators often fail to take account of the difference between these two aspects of proficiency when they teach and assess minority students. For example, in the Cummins (1984) study, it was found that because students often appeared to be fluent in English, psychologists tended to assume that they had overcome all problems in learning English and consequently IQ tests administered in English were valid. The data clearly showed that this assumption was unfounded. Students were frequently labelled as "learning disabled" or "retarded" on the basis of tests administered within one or two years of the students' exposure to English in school. In fact, the research data show that even students who had been instructed through English for three years in school were performing at the equivalent of 15 IQ points below grade norms as a direct result of insufficient time to catch up with their native English-speaking peers (Cummins, 1981, 1984).

The same logic applies to the exiting of minority students prematurely to all-English programs. Educators frequently assume that students are ready to survive without support in an all-English classroom on the basis of the fact that they appear to be fluent in English. This surface fluency may mask significant gaps in the development of academic aspects of English. The result is that after premature exit from the bilingual program, the student performs considerably below grade level in the regular classroom.

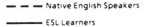

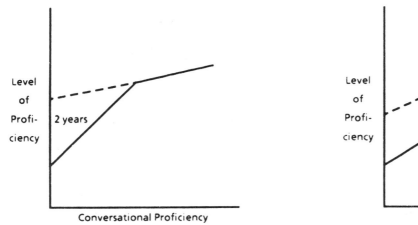
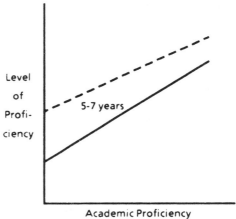

Figure 3-1 Length of Time Required to
Achieve Age-Appropriate Levels of
Conversational and Academic Language Proficiency

The fact that minority students may require upwards of five years to catch up to native-English-speaking students in English academic skills does not, in itself, necessarily imply that these students should be in withdrawal ESL or bilingual classes for this period. It does imply, however, that instruction in mainstream classes after students have been exited from ESL or bilingual programs must be tuned to students' level of English in order to provide them with the comprehensible input necessary to sustain academic growth (Krashen, 1981; Wong Fillmore, 1983). In addition, academic growth will be fostered by context-embedded instruction that validates students' background experiences by encouraging them to express, share, and amplify these experiences (see Chapters 5 and 6).

In short, the research evidence suggests that although there are large individual differences between children in the rapidity with which they acquire different aspects of English proficiency (Wong Fillmore, 1983), verbal tests of psychological functioning or achievement tend to underestimate minority students' academic potential until they have been learning the school language for *at least* 4-5 years.

Another implication of these findings is that for students who have been learning the school language for less than this period, it becomes extremely problematic to attempt any diagnosis of categories such as "learning disability" since any genuine learning problems are likely to be masked by as yet inadequately developed proficiency in the school language. The unresolved problems inherent in disentangling the assessment of language and academic skills among minority students can be seen in the fact that, in Texas, Hispanic students are still over-represented by a factor of 300% in the "learning disabilities" category (Ortiz and Yates, 1983).

The Conversational/Academic Language Proficiency Principle

The evidence presented above suggests the importance of distinguishing children's ability to function conversationally in English from their ability to function academically in English. Academic uses of language often require the ability to manipulate language without the support provided in an interpersonal communicative context (e.g. negotiation of meaning, immediate feedback, etc).

This distinction is a convenient and, I believe, important one. However, any dichotomy inevitably oversimplifies the reality. Thus, it is appropriate to clarify certain aspects of the distinction. First, it refers not to two totally separate aspects of language functioning but to a continuum of uses of language that children gradually acquire as they develop during the preschool and school years. The conversational/academic continuum is not identical to the distinction between oral and written uses of language.

Written uses do tend to require explicit and decontextualized use of language, since the communicative partner is not present and a shared context often cannot be assumed, but many oral language interactions, both in school and outside school, are also decontextualized to a greater or lesser extent and thus would be characterized as "academic" (see Biber, 1986, for an intriguing investigation of these issues). A central aspect of what I have termed "academic" language proficiency is the ability to make complex meanings explicit in either oral or written modalities by means of *language itself* rather than by means of paralinguistic cues (e.g. gestures, intonation etc). Experience of these uses of language in oral interactions prior to school clearly helps to prepare children to use and understand the increasingly decontextualized language demands of school.

Similar distinctions have been made by a number of other investigators (see Cummins, 1984 for a review). Snow (1983), for example, distinguishes between contextualized and decontextualized language and argues that exposure to decontextualized language use at home is an important predictor of academic success at school. In a study of approximately 150 English-French bilingual children in grades 2-5, Snow, Cancino, Gonzalez and Shriberg (1987) reported a strong relationship between children's ability to give formal definitions of words and their performance on a standardized reading test. Foley (1987) has reported similar results in a case study of successful and unsuccessful Spanish-English bilingual readers.

On the basis of her extensive ethnographic study among middle-class and lower-class families, Heath (1983) argues that the differences between social classes in learning to read derives from more than just differential access to literacy materials at home. What is more significant is the extent to which literacy activities are integrated with children's daily lives. The black and white *Maintown* (middle-class) children in her study experienced activities such as inventing narratives related to the stories that were read to them and comparing book characters with real people they knew. They learned to view language as an artifact separate from its use in face-to-face communicative contexts.

Heath (1986) enumerates some of the ways in which schools expect children to be able to use language before they begin formal schooling:

1. Use language to label and describe the objects, events and information that non-intimates present to them;

2. Use language to recount in a predictable order and format past events or information given to them by non-intimates;

3. Follow directions from oral and written sources without needing sustained personal reinforcement from adults or peers;

4. Use language to sustain and maintain the social interactions of the group;

5. Use language to obtain and clarify information from non-intimates;

6. Use language on appropriate occasions to account for one's unique experiences, to link these to generally known ideas or events, and to create new information or to integrate ideas in innovative ways.

Heath points out that those students who achieve academic success either bring to school all of these language uses, and the cultural norms that lie behind them, or they learn quickly to intuit the rules of these language uses for both speaking and writing. Minority children who have these functions of language available in their L1 can transfer them easily to English, given appropriate opportunities in English (see Chapter 4). Thus, both in-school and out-of-school occasions (in both L1 and L2) that require explanation of facts and assumptions not shared by others provide practice in the kind of decontextualized and impersonal language that is important for academic success. Heath suggests, for example, that a child who listens to a bank teller explain to her mother the rules for opening a savings account learns something about how to present information to someone who does not already share it, a use of language that will be invoked in much of the child's writing in school.

The relevance for academic success of these competencies in varied uses of language can be seen from the fact that as students progress through the grades, they are increasingly required to manipulate language in cognitively-demanding and decontextualized situations that differ significantly from everyday conversational interactions. In writing, for example, they must learn to continue to produce language without the prompting that comes from a conversational partner and they must plan large units of discourse, and organize them coherently, rather than planning only what will be said next.

It is important for educators to realize that children come to school with different degrees of exposure to decontextualized language. When students have had little exposure to such uses of language prior to school and instruction in school assumes that these uses have been developed already, the resulting "mismatch" can cause considerable initial confusion for children. This mismatch in the pragmatic or functional aspects of language is very different from the "linguistic mismatch" referred to in Chapter 2. The latter mismatch entails a switch between the language of the home (e.g. Spanish) and the language of the school (English) and is not *in itself* a major cause of academic problems for minority students. However, "pragmatic mismatches" in the ways of using language (as discussed by Heath [1983] and Snow [1983]) are potentially more serious causes of difficulty for minority students. The potential for such mismatches is minimized when initial instruction in school is highly context-embedded or "interactive/experiential" (see Chapter 5).[3]

In short, the notion of "academic" aspects of language proficiency involves a complex array of linguistic competencies that are discussed in more detail elsewhere (e.g. Cummins and Swain, 1986; Heath, 1983; Lindfors, 1980; Snow, 1983). For purposes of this monograph, it is sufficient to emphasize that the general distinction between conversational and academic aspects of language proficiency (or contextualized and decontextualized uses of language) carries important implications for the education of language minority students.

Conclusion

As discussed in Chapter 2, minority students' educational failure cannot be attributed solely to linguistic factors. However, misconceptions about language on the part of educators have clearly contributed to students' difficulties; in fact, it is argued in Chapter 5 that the persistence of these misconceptions about language is a *symptom* of the underlying educational structure that disables minority students. For educators, a first step in becoming conscious of the ways in which this underlying structure operates to promote discriminatory assessment, placement and instruction of minority students is to critically examine the notion of "language proficiency" and how it affects performance on psychometric tests. Specifically, it is necessary to acknowledge that students' surface fluency in English cannot be taken as indicative of their overall proficiency in

---

[3]Among the communication activities in school that provide students with opportunities to develop decontextualized uses of language in meaningful contexts are many kinds of cooperative learning activities (see Kagan, 1986). The same goal is also achieved by *barrier games*. In this type of activity children work in pairs and each member of a pair is given a picture or object that the other child cannot see because of a barrier (e.g. a low cardboard screen) put up between the two children. The partners then talk to each other to determine differences and similarities between the two pictures. A variation is to have one child draw a picture related to a particular topic and then describe the picture to her partner who attempts to draw the picture as it is described (see New Zealand Department of Education, 1988, for further excellent examples that can be used to promote communication skills among both minority and non-minority students).

English. Similarly, ESL teachers and bilingual educators should realize that their task is to develop *academic* skills in English, not just conversational skills. Academic skills in English usually require most of the elementary school years to develop to grade norms, and, as discussed in the following chapter, are more dependent on children's conceptual foundation in L1 than on their English conversational fluency.[4]

It is also crucial for educators and policy-makers to face up to the implications for intervention of the fact that children are not failing in school because of lack of English fluency. Lack of English fluency may be a secondary contributor to children's academic difficulty but the fundamental causal factors of both success and failure lie in what is communicated to children in their interactions with educators. This is clearly expressed by Isidro Lucas (1981) in describing a research study he carried out in the early 1970's with Puerto Rican students in Chicago designed to explore the reasons for student dropout. Although he prepared questionnaires in both Spanish and English, he never had to use the Spanish version. The reason was that

> "All my dropout respondents spoke good understandable English. They hadn't learned math, or social sciences, or natural sciences, unfortunately. But they had learned English ... No dropout mentioned lack of English as the reason for quitting. As it evolved through questionnaires and interviews, theirs was a more subtle story - of alienation, of not belonging, of being 'push-outs' ... To my surprise, dropouts expressed more confidence in their ability to speak English than did the stay-ins (seniors in high school). For their part, stay-ins showed more confidence in their Spanish than did dropouts ... I had to conclude that identity, expressed in one's confidence and acceptance of the native culture, was more a determinant of school stay-in power than the mere acquisition of the coding-decoding skills involved in a different language, English" (p. 19).

In short, understanding why and how minority students are failing academically requires that educators dig a little deeper than superficial linguistic mismatches between home and school or insufficient exposure to

---

[4]It is emphasized in subsequent chapters that the distinction between conversational and academic aspects of language proficiency does *not* imply that academic skills should be developed through decontextualized instruction. On the contrary, high levels of literacy and critical thinking can be promoted effectively only by interactive/experiential instruction that encourages students' oral and written expression.

English. Underachievement is not caused by lack of fluency in English. Underachievement is the result of particular kinds of interactions in school that lead minority students to mentally withdraw from academic effort. The nature of these interactions is explored in Chapters 4 and 5.

CHAPTER 4

DOUBLE-TALK AND DOUBLE-THINK: BILINGUALISM AND CHILDREN'S DEVELOPMENT IN SCHOOL

Despite the fact that issues surrounding the education of language minority students in the United States have been highly controversial and emotionally charged for almost twenty years, there still appears to be little consensus among policy-makers and educators about what programs and teaching practices are appropriate. This is surprising in view of the considerable amount of research on bilingualism and bilingual education that has been carried out in many countries.

I argue in this chapter that there *is* an empirical and theoretical basis for educational policy-decisions in this area. In other words, a psychoeducational knowledge base exists whereby policy-makers can predict, with considerable accuracy, at least some of the outcomes of different types of programs in a wide variety of contexts.

The Policy Debate: Assumptions Underlying the "Immersion" Versus "Bilingual Education" Issue

In recent years, what has variously been called "immersion" or "structured immersion" has been promoted by some policy-makers and researchers as a viable alternative to transitional bilingual education for language minority students (see Baker & de Kanter, 1981; Dunn, 1987; Gersten and Woodward, 1985a, 1985b). Structured immersion programs essentially consist of all-English programs in which minority students are "immersed" in English with some special steps (e.g. ESL instruction) taken to help them acquire English. Immersion programs have been strenuously opposed by proponents of bilingual education who argue that many so-called immersion programs are little more than "sink-or-swim" or "submersion" (Cohen & Swain, 1976) programs that, in reality, provide little assistance to minority students to acquire academic competence in the language of instruction.

These arguments about the relative merits of different programs reflect very different theoretical assumptions about the relationship between second language development and academic achievement. By a "theoretical assumption" I mean a set of hypotheses from which predictions can be made about program outcomes in different contexts. Research findings by themselves cannot be directly generalized across contexts. For example, knowing that a maintenance bilingual program for Navajo students in Rock Point, Arizona, resulted in students performing at national norms in English academic skills (Rosier and Holm, 1980) does not, in itself, imply that a similar approach would be effective in a different context. Theories, on the other hand, are almost by definition applicable across contexts since the adequacy of a particular theory or hypothesis is assessed precisely by how well it can account for research findings derived from a variety of sociocultural contexts. If the theory cannot account for the data then it is inadequate and requires revision.

As outlined in Chapter 2, two opposing theoretical assumptions have dominated the U.S. policy debate regarding the effectiveness of bilingual education in promoting minority students' academic achievement. These assumptions are essentially hypotheses regarding the causes of minority students' academic failure and each is associated with a particular form of educational intervention designed to reverse this failure. In support of transitional bilingual education where some initial instruction is given in students' first language (L1), it is argued that students cannot learn in a language they do not understand; thus, a home-school language switch will almost inevitably result in academic retardation unless initial content is taught through L1 while students are acquiring English. In other words, minority students' academic difficulties are attributed to a "linguistic mismatch" between home and school.

The opposing argument is that if minority students are deficient in English, then they need as much exposure to English as possible. Students' academic difficulties are attributed to insufficient exposure to English in the home and environment. Thus, bilingual programs which reduce this exposure to English even further appear illogical and counterproductive in that they seem to imply that less exposure to English will lead to more English achievement.

Viewed as theoretical principles from which predictions regarding program outcomes can be derived, the "linguistic mismatch" and "insufficient exposure" hypotheses are each patently inadequate. The linguistic mismatch assumption would predict that a home-school language switch will inevitably result in academic difficulties. This prediction is refuted by a considerable amount of research data from Canada and other countries showing that, under certain conditions, children exposed to a home-school language switch experience no academic retardation. The Canadian data involve programs that immerse English background students in French (L2) as a means of developing a high level of bilingual and biliteracy skills. Initial academic instruction is through French and by the end of elementary school approximately 50% of instructional time is spent through each language. In other words, these programs are fully *bilingual*, even though initial instruction is through students' second language. However, the teacher is always bilingual and can understand everything that children say to her/him in their L1. Currently about 230,000 Canadian students are in various forms of French immersion programs. These programs have been evaluated as highly successful in developing French proficiency at no cost to English (L1) academic skills (Swain & Lapkin, 1982). This pattern of findings is clearly inconsistent with what the linguistic mismatch hypothesis would predict. Similarly, the success of a considerable number of minority students under home-school language switch conditions refutes the linguistic mismatch hypothesis. In short, the usual rationale for bilingual education cannot fully account for the research data and thus provides an inadequate basis for policy decisions with respect to language minority students.

However, the "insufficient exposure" hypothesis fares no better. Virtually every bilingual program that has ever been evaluated (including French immersion programs) shows that students instructed through a minority language for all or part of the school day perform, over time, at least as well in the majority language (e.g. English in North America) as students instructed exclusively through the majority language (See Cummins, 1984; Hakuta, 1986 for reviews). In other words, students in, for example, a Spanish-English bilingual program (or a French immersion program) do not lose out in the development of English academic skills despite spending considerably less time through English than comparable students instructed entirely through English. In fact, as discussed below, these students frequently perform considerably better in bilingual programs than in all-English programs.

In summary, the policy debate on bilingual programs in the United States has not been particularly well-informed with respect to the research data. There is, however, a considerable amount of research relevant to the policy issues and two theoretical principles that can account for the pattern of research findings regarding bilingualism and bilingual education are reviewed below. First, however, the important policy issue of the extent to which bilingual programs are effective in promoting minority students' academic development is examined.

Are Bilingual Education Programs Effective?

It has been suggested above that the causes of minority students' difficulties are rooted in much more than just a linguistic mismatch between home and school. Linguistic factors alone are not capable of explaining the varied academic performance of different minority groups nor the apparent success of middle-class majority students exposed to a home-school linguistic mismatch.

Consideration of historical and social factors (Chapter 2) suggested that the extent to which the school reflects the power relations in the broader society has played a major role in minority students' academic development. Specifically, in the past, the school has overtly reinforced the cultural insecurity and ambivalence that some minority communities appear to experience, thereby contributing to students' "mental withdrawal" (Carter, 1970) from academic effort.

This analysis entails several hypotheses regarding the effects of different forms of educational interventions. For example, it predicts that bilingual education programs will vary in their outcomes depending upon the extent to which students' primary language is genuinely promoted and community participation is encouraged. Assessment and pedagogical practices that provide students with a sense of academic and personal efficacy will also tend to be associated with educational success. In other words, bilingual programs would be expected to have varied effects depending upon the extent to which they explicitly attempt to reverse the pattern of dominant-dominated power relations in the society at large. However, we would also predict that bilingual programs, as a whole, would tend to show better results than monolingual programs because of the probability that at least in some of these programs minority students' cultural identity and primary language skills are promoted to a greater extent than is the case in monolingual programs. These predictions are examined below.

A recent meta-analysis (Willig, 1985) of bilingual education studies suggests that, overall, there is evidence that bilingual programs are more successful than English-only programs:

> "When statistical controls for methodological inadequacies were employed, participation in bilingual education programs consistently produced small to moderate differences favoring bilingual education for tests of reading, language skills, mathematics, and total achievement when the tests were in English, and for reading, language, mathematics, writing, social studies, listening comprehension, and attitudes toward school or self when tests were in other languages" (Willig, 1985, p. 269).

In-depth studies of particular bilingual programs that have explicitly attempted to develop full bilingualism among Hispanic students and to involve Hispanic parents in promoting their children's education (e.g. California State Department of Education, 1985; Campos and Keatinge, 1988) show dramatic gains in students' academic performance, demonstrating that bilingual programs can be highly effective in reversing the pattern of minority students' academic failure. Campos and Keatinge (1988), for example, reported that Hispanic children enrolled in a Spanish-only preschool program learned more English and developed considerably more academic readiness skills than comparable children enrolled in a Head Start bilingual preschool where the emphasis was on promoting English proficiency. Krashen and Biber (1987) have also recently reviewed the results of several bilingual programs in California in which minority students approach grade norms during the elementary school years and surpass the performance of similar students in English-only programs (see also Crawford, 1988, for an excellent review of recent research and theory).

These data clearly show that less English instruction *can* result in *more* English academic skills development. The data also refute the assumptions underlying the call for "English immersion" programs since they show an inverse relationship between the amount of English in the program and students' achievement in English. Virtually all the evaluation findings from bilingual education programs in North America, Europe, Africa and Asia show a similar pattern of either no relationship or an inverse relationship between exposure to the majority language in school and achievement in that language. Thus, it is difficult to understand the frequent claim that research data on bilingual education are lacking; rather, what has been lacking is a rational process of examining the research data in relation to the predictions derived from theory. If predictions derived from the "linguistic mismatch" and "insufficient exposure" assumptions had been examined, their inadequacy for policy would have been apparent. The lack of rational policy analysis suggests that the call for English immersion programs is more strongly based on political than on pedagogical considerations.

This conclusion is supported by preliminary results from a large-scale comparative evaluation of immersion and bilingual education programs (see Crawford, 1986). The study in question involves about 4,000 students and is being carried out for the U.S. Department of Education by SRA Technologies Inc. The early results were reported in Education Week (1986, 5, no. 30, April 23) as follows:

> "English immersion, an instructional alternative that is popular among critics of bilingual education, has fared poorly in the U.S. Education Department's first large-scale evaluation of the method, according to early results. ... limited-English-proficient students in bilingual programs consistently outperformed "immersion strategy" students in reading, language-arts, and mathematics tests conducted in both English and Spanish. ... Especially perplexing to the S.R.A. researchers

was the poor English-language performance of the immersion students, who had received the most English-language instruction. Moreover, the larger the native-language component of their schooling, the better the students performed in English. ... researchers determined that the immersion classes used English 90 percent of the time, compared with 67 percent in the early-exit bilingual programs and 33 percent in the late-exit bilingual programs. Overall test scores from five school districts showed an inverse relation between English-language exposure and English-language proficiency among kindergartners and 1st graders" (Crawford, 1986, p. 1 and 10).[1]

How can we account for the pattern of research findings? Why is it that less exposure to English often appears to result in greater development of English academic skills? Sociopolitical and historical reasons for this are considered in the next chapter. However, there are also psychoeducational factors at work. Two psychoeducational principles that are supported by a broad array of research evidence are useful in accounting for the research data on bilingualism and bilingual education. These are the "additive bilingualism enrichment" principle and the "interdependence" principle.

The Additive Bilingualism Enrichment Principle

In the past many students from minority backgrounds have experienced difficulties in school and have performed at a lower level than monolingual children on verbal IQ tests and on measures of literacy development. As outlined in Table 2-1 (Chapter 2), these findings led researchers in the period between 1920 and 1960 to speculate that bilingualism caused language handicaps and cognitive confusion among children. Some research studies also reported that bilingual children suffered emotional conflicts more frequently than monolingual children. Thus, in the early part of this century bilingualism acquired a doubtful reputation among educators, and many schools redoubled their efforts to eradicate minority children's first language on the grounds that this language was the source of children's academic difficulties.

However, virtually all of the early research involved minority students who were in the process of replacing their L1 with the majority language, usually with strong encouragement from the school. Many minority

---

[1]At the time of writing (December 1988), the final report of this project has not been published nor have there been any further leaks to the media regarding the results.

students in North America were physically punished for speaking their L1 in school. Thus, these students usually failed to develop adequate literacy skills in this language and many also experienced academic and emotional difficulty in school. This, however, was not because of bilingualism but rather because of the treatment they received in schools which essentially amounted to an assault on their personal identities.

More recent studies suggest that far from being a negative force in children's personal and academic development, bilingualism can positively affect both intellectual and linguistic progress. A large number of studies have reported that bilingual children exhibit a greater sensitivity to linguistic meanings and may be more flexible in their thinking than are monolingual children (Cummins, 1984; Hakuta, 1986). Most of these studies have investigated aspects of children's metalinguistic development; in other words, children's explicit knowledge about the structure and functions of language itself.

In general, it is not surprising that bilingual children should be more adept at certain aspects of linguistic processing. In gaining control over two language systems, the bilingual child has had to decipher much more language input than the monolingual child who has been exposed to only one language system. Thus, the bilingual child has had considerably more practice in analysing meanings than the monolingual child.

The evidence is not conclusive as to whether this linguistic advantage transfers to more general cognitive skills; McLaughlin's review of the literature, for example, concludes that:

> It seems clear that the child who has mastered two languages has a linguistic advantage over the the monolingual child. Bilingual children become aware that there are two ways of saying the same thing. But does this sensitivity to the lexical and formal aspects of language generalize to cognitive functioning? There is no conclusive answer to this question - mainly because it has proven so difficult to apply the necessary controls in research (1984, p. 44).

Hakuta and Diaz (1985) and Diaz (1986) have attempted to overcome the problems of comparing bilingual and monolingual groups by following more than 300 Spanish dominant Puerto Rican elementary school children in the bilingual education program in New Haven public schools. They related students' developing bilingualism to nonverbal intelligence (as measured by Raven's Progressive Matrices) and to metalinguistic awareness. The students' Spanish performance reflected their verbal ability in their native language while their English proficiency reflected their degree of bilingualism. English skills were found to be significantly related to cognitive and, to a lesser extent, metalinguistic abilities. Further analyses suggested that if bilingualism and cognitive ability are causally related, bilingualism is most likely the causal factor. Hakuta (1986), however, cautions that even this carefully controlled study does not provide unambiguous support for bilingualism affecting general cognitive abilities. It may be that English and nonverbal ability are related because English is the skill that children are concentrating on learning in school and nonverbal ability is related to overall success in school.

An important characteristic of the bilingual children in the more recent studies (conducted since the early 1960's) is that, for the most part, they were developing what has been termed an *additive* form of bilingualism (Lambert, 1975); in other words, they were adding a second language to their repertory of skills at no cost to the development of their first language. Consequently, these children were in the process of attaining a relatively high level of both fluency and literacy in their two languages. The children in these studies tended to come either from majority language groups whose first language was strongly reinforced in the society (e.g. English-speakers in French immersion programs) or from minority groups whose first languages were reinforced by bilingual programs in the school. Minority children who lack this educational support for literacy development in L1 frequently develop a *subtractive* form of bilingualism in which L1 skills are replaced by L2.

This pattern of findings suggests that the level of proficiency attained by bilingual students in their two languages may be an important influence on their academic and intellectual development (Cummins, 1979). Specifically, there may be a threshold level of proficiency in both languages which students must attain in order to avoid any negative academic consequences and a second, higher, threshold necessary to reap the linguistic and possibly intellectual benefits of bilingualism and biliteracy.

Diaz (1986) has questioned the threshold hypothesis on the grounds that the effects of bilingualism on cognitive abilities in his data were stronger for children of relatively low L2 proficiency (non-balanced bilinguals). This suggests that the positive effects are related to the initial struggles and experiences of the beginning second-language learner. This interpretation does not appear to be incompatible with the threshold hypothesis since the major point of this hypothesis is that for positive effects to manifest themselves, children must be in the process of developing high levels of bilingual skills. If beginning L2 learners do not continue to develop both their languages, any initial positive effects are likely to be counteracted by the negative consequences of subtractive bilingualism.

One wheel can get you places....

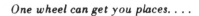

So can a big wheel and a little wheel....

However, when your wheels are nicely balanced and fully inflated you'll go further....

Provided, of course, the people who made the wheels knew what they were doing....

In summary, the conclusion that emerges from the research on the academic, linguistic and intellectual effects of bilingualism can be stated thus:

> The development of additive bilingual and biliteracy skills entails no negative consequences for children's academic, linguistic, or intellectual development. On the contrary, although not conclusive, the evidence points in the direction of subtle metalinguistic, academic and intellectual benefits for bilingual children.

The Linguistic Interdependence Principle

The fact that there is little relationship between amount of instructional time through the majority language and academic achievement in that language strongly suggests that first and second language academic skills are interdependent, i.e., manifestations of a common underlying proficiency. The interdependence principle has been stated formally as follows (Cummins, 1981b, p. 29):

> To the extent that instruction in Lx is effective in promoting proficiency in Lx, transfer of this proficiency to Ly will occur provided there is adequate exposure to Ly (either in school or environment) and adequate motivation to learn Ly.

In concrete terms, what this principle means is that in, for example, a Spanish-English bilingual program, Spanish instruction that develops Spanish reading and writing skills (for either Spanish L1 or L2 speakers) is not just developing *Spanish* skills, it is also developing a deeper conceptual and linguistic proficiency that is strongly related to the development of literacy in the majority language (English). In other words, although the surface aspects (e.g. pronunciation, fluency, etc.) of different languages are clearly separate, there is an underlying cognitive/academic proficiency which is common across languages. This "common underlying proficiency" makes possible the transfer of cognitive/academic or literacy-related skills across languages. Transfer is much more likely to occur from minority to majority language because of the greater exposure to literacy in the majority language outside of school and the strong social pressure to learn it. The interdependence principle is depicted in Figure 4-1.

A recent review of bilingual education policy carried out by the Association for Supervision and Curriculum Development (ASCD) expresses the interdependence of bilingual language proficiency as follows:

"Having a strong foundation in the native language makes learning a second language both easier and faster. ... Moreover, there is general agreement that knowledge transfers readily from one language to another, so that students do not have to relearn in a second language what they have already learned in a first. In fact, it is clear that the ability to transfer to English what is learned in the native language applies not only to content-area subjects like science and math, but also to skills in reading and writing - even when the orthographic system is quite different from the Roman alphabet ..." (1987, p. 22).

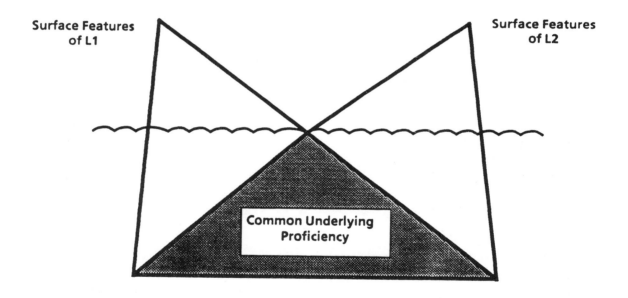

Figure 4-1 THE LINGUISTIC INTERDEPENDENCE MODEL

A considerable amount of evidence supporting the interdependence principle has been reviewed by Cummins (1983, 1984) and Cummins and Swain (1986). The results of virtually all evaluations of bilingual programs for both majority and minority students are consistent with predictions derived from the interdependence principle (see Cummins, 1983). The interdependence principle is also capable of accounting for data on immigrant students' L2 acquisition (e.g. Cummins, 1981c) as well as from studies of bilingual language use in the home (e.g. Bhatnagar, 1980; Dolson, 1985). Correlational studies also consistently reveal a strong degree of cognitive/academic interdependence across languages.

Recent studies continue to support the interdependence principle. Kemp (1984), for example, reported that Hebrew (L1) cognitive/academic abilities accounted for 48% of the variance in English (L2) acadmic skills among 196 seventh grade Israeli students. Treger and Wong (1984) reported significant positive relationships between L1 and English reading abilities (measured by cloze tests) among both Hispanic and Chinese-background elementary school students in Boston. In other words, students above grade level in their first language reading also tended to be above grade level for English reading. Snow et al. (1987) in a study involving about 150 English-French bilingual children, reported significant positive correlations between decontextualized language skills in the two languages.

Two longitudinal studies also provide strong support for the notion of linguistic interdependence. Ramirez (1985) followed 75 Hispanic elementary school students in Newark, New Jersey, enrolled in bilingual programs for three years. It was found that Spanish and English academic language scores loaded on one single factor over the three years of data collection. This factor was interpreted as a cognitive/academic dimension that underlies students' conceptual development in both languages.

Hakuta and Diaz (1985) with a similar sample of Hispanic students found an increasing correlation between English and Spanish academic skills over time. Between Kindergarten and third grade the correlation between English and Spanish went from 0 to .68. The low cross-lingual relationship at the Kindergarten level is likely due to the varied length of residence of the students and their parents in the United States which would result in varying levels of English proficiency at the start of school.

A series of case studies of five schools attempting to implement the Theoretical Framework developed by the California State Department of Education (1981) showed consistently higher correlations between English and Spanish reading skills (range $r = .60-.74$) than between English reading and English oral language skills (range r = .36-.59) (California State Department of Education, 1985). In these analyses scores were broken down by months in the program (1-12 months through 73-84). It was also found that the relation between L1 and L2 reading became stronger as English oral communicative skills grew stronger (r = .71, N = 190 for students in the highest category of English oral skills).

Recently, Geva and Ryan (1987) have reported evidence with Hebrew-English bilinguals in Toronto that L1 cognitive/academic skills are significantly related to L2 cognitive/academic skills. They show that not only underlying non-verbal intellectual factors are involved in this process but also memory storage capacity and analytic processes required in performing academic tasks. In other words, they have made explicit some of the cognitive processes that are involved in mediating the transfer from L1 to L2.

A well-controlled study of cross-lingual relationships in writing development (Carlisle, 1986) reported that Hispanic students' rhetorical effectiveness in Spanish was a significant predictor of rhetorical effectiveness in English. Carlisle also reported that when controls for background factors were taken into account, Hispanic fourth and sixth grade students in a bilingual program performed significantly better on English writing productivity, syntactic maturity, and rhetorical effectiveness than did Hispanic students in a submersion program.

European research also supports the interdependence hypothesis. McLaughlin (1986), for example, reviewed research carried out by German linguist Jochen Rehbein (1984) which found that

> "the ability of Turkish children to deal with complex texts in German was affected by their ability to understand these texts in their first language. Rehbein's investigations suggest that there is a strong developmental interrelationship between the bilingual child's two languages and that conceptual information and discourse strategies acquired in the first language transfer to the second" (1986, p. 34-35).

McLaughlin goes on to compare the principle of linguistic interdependence to the Soviet notion of "set" which is a general competence that underlies both languages of a bilingual. He describes "set" as

> "some unconscious 'feel' for language that permits its practical use in communicative settings. It is this competence in the first language that provides the basis for second-language learning"

(1986, p. 44).

Thus, in Soviet education, the teaching of Russian to linguistic minority groups is based on strong promotion of children's first language in the early years of schooling, and additive bilingualism is the goal (McLaughlin, 1986).

Finally, Cummins, Harley, Swain and Allen (in press) have reported highly significant correlations for written grammatical, discourse and sociolinguistic skills in Portuguese (L1) and English (L2) among Portuguese grade 7 students in Toronto. Cross-language correlations for oral skills were generally not significant. Significant cross-linguistic relationships for reading and writing skills were also observed among Japanese-background students in the Cummins et al. study. The same pattern of linguistic interdependence has also been reported in other recent studies (e.g. Goldman, 1984; Guerra, 1984; Katsaiti, 1983).

In conclusion, the research evidence shows consistent support for the principle of linguistic interdependence in studies investigating a variety of issues (e.g. bilingual education, memory functioning of bilinguals, age and second language learning, bilingual reading skills etc) and using different methodologies. The research has also been carried out in a wide variety of sociopolitical contexts. The consistency and strength of support indicates that highly reliable policy predictions can be made on the basis of this principle. In other words, unlike the "linguistic mismatch" and "insufficient exposure" hypotheses, the interdependence principle *can* account for the research data on bilingual programs for both minority and majority children.

The Interdependence Principle and Second Language Acquisition

Most second language theorists (e.g. Krashen, 1981; 1982; Long, 1983; Schacter, 1983; Wong Fillmore, 1983) currently endorse some form of the "input" hypothesis which essentially states that acquisition of a second language depends not just on exposure to the language but on access to second language input that is modified in various ways to make it comprehensible. Krashen, in fact, argues that comprehensible input is *the* primary causal variable in second language acquisition. Underlying the notion of comprehensible input is the obvious fact that a central function of language use is meaningful communication; when this central function of language is ignored in classroom instruction, learning is likely to be by rote and supported only by extrinsic motivation.

One important link between the interdependence principle and the notion of comprehensible input is that knowledge (e.g. subject matter content, literacy skills, etc) acquired through linguistic interaction in one languge plays a major role in making input in the other language comprehensible (Cummins, 1984; Krashen, 1981). For example, an immigrant student who already has the concept of "honesty" in her or his first language will require considerably less input in the second language containing the term to acquire its meaning than will a student who does not already know the concept. A new label needs to be acquired, not a new concept. In the same way, the first language conceptual knowledge developed in bilingual programs for minority students greatly facilitates the acquisition of L2 literacy and subject matter content. The more background knowledge we have, the more capable we are of understanding and internalizing new input.

Conclusion

This review of psychoeducational data regarding bilingual academic development shows that a theoretical and research basis for at least some policy decisions regarding minority students' education dues exist. In other words, policy-makers can predict with considerable reliability the probable effects of educational programs for minority students implemented in very different sociopolitical contexts.

First, they can be confident that if the program is effective in continuning to develop students' academic skills in both languages, no cognitive confusion or handicap will result; in fact, students may benefit in subtle ways from access to two linguistic systems.

Second, they can be confident that spending instructional time through the minority language will not result in lower levels of academic performance in the majority language, provided of course, the instructional program is effective in developing academic skills in the minority language. This is because at deeper levels of conceptual and academic functioning, there is considerable overlap or interdependence across languages. Conceptual knowledge developed in one language helps to make input in the other language comprehensible.

These two psychoeducational principles open up significant possibilities for the planning of bilingual programs by showing that, when programs are well-implemented, students will not suffer academically either as a result of bilingualism *per se* or as a result of spending less instructional time through English. If academic development of minority students is the goal, then students must be encouraged to acquire a conceptual foundation in their L1 to facilitate the acquisition of English academic skills.

However, these psychoeducational principles, by themselves, do not constitute a fully adequate basis for planning educational interventions for minority students who are academically at risk or who come from groups that have been characterized by persistent school failure. The psychoeducational principles do not address the fundamental causes of minority children's educational difficulties, which, as noted in Chapter 2, are sociopolitical and sociohistorical in nature. Also, they do not fully account for the fact that, under some circumstances, bilingual programs have been dramatically successful in reversing children's academic difficulties. Thus, a theoretical framework for intervention is required that takes account of the interactions between sociopolitical and psychoeducational factors and that is capable of predicting the probable outcomes of different types of program for minority students. An intervention framework for empowering minority students is outlined in the next chapter.

CHAPTER 5

TOWARDS ANTI-RACIST EDUCATION: EMPOWERING
MINORITY STUDENTS

During the past twenty years educators in the United States have implemented a series of costly reforms aimed at reversing the pattern of school failure among minority students. These have included compensatory programs at the preschool level, myriad forms of bilingual education programs, the hiring of additional aides and remedial personnel, and the institution of safeguards against discriminatory assessment procedures. Yet the dropout rate among Mexican-American and mainland Puerto Rican students remains between 40 and 50 percent compared to 14 percent for Whites and 25 percent for Blacks (Jusenius and Duarte, 1982) and overrepresentation in special education classes continues (Ortiz and Yates, 1983).

In this chapter, I examine some of the reasons why the rhetoric of "educational equity" has failed to translate into reality. The basic argument presented is that the goal of equality of educational opportunity can be realized only when policy-makers, educators and communities acknowledge the subtle (and sometimes not so subtle) forms of institutionalized discrimination that permeate the structure of schools and mediate the interactions between educators and students.[1] In other words, unless it becomes "anti-racist education," "bilingual education" may serve only to provide a veneer of change that in reality perpetuates discriminatory educational structures.

These discriminatory structures are manifested in the *interactions* that minority students and communities experience with *individual* educators. Since schools reflect the societies that support them, it is hardly surprising that these interactions reflect the power relations in the society at large. Previous attempts at educational reform have been largely unsuccessful because the relationships between teachers and students and between schools and communities have remained largely unchanged. Educators have uncritically (and in most cases unconsciously) accepted rather than challenged the societal discrimination that is reflected in schools.

---

[1]The term "anti-racist education" is being increasingly used in many educational contexts (e.g. Britain, Canada) to refer to educational initiatives that challenge the overt and covert racism that is often embedded in the structure and hidden curriculum of schools. For examples of anti-racist initiatives in the area of science teaching see Gill and Levidow (1987).

A central assumption of the present analysis is that implementation of anti-racist educational changes requires *personal redefinitions* of the ways in which classroom teachers and other educators interact with the children and communities they serve. In other words, legislative and policy reforms may be necessary conditions for effective change, but they are not sufficient. Implementation of change is dependent on the extent to which educators, both collectively and individually, redefine their roles with respect to minority students and communities. This process of role redefinition involves a commitment to *empower* minority children, both personally and academically, rather than just transmit a body of knowledge and skills.

The chapter is organized as follows: first, the meaning of the term "institutionalized racism" is discussed and a concrete example of its operation is presented. Then the sociohistorical and psychoeducational data reviewed in previous chapters are examined within the context of a theoretical framework for empowering minority students. This framework analyses the ways in which educators define their roles with respect to four overlapping dimensions of schooling: (a) incorporation of minority students' language and culture; (b) minority community participation; (c) orientation to pedagogy; and (d) assessment of minority students.

From Overt to Covert Racism

Institutionalized racism can be defined as ideologies and structures which are used to systematically legitimize unequal division of power and resources between groups which are defined on the basis of race (see Skutnabb-Kangas and Cummins, 1988). The term "racism" is being used here in a broad sense to include discrimination against both ethnic and racial minorities.[2] The discrimination is brought about both by the ways particular institutions (e.g. schools) are organized or structured and by the (usually) implicit assumptions that legitimize that organization. There is usually no intent to discriminate on the part of educators; however, their interactions with minority students are mediated by a system of unquestioned assumptions that reflect the values and priorities of the

---

[2] the term "institutionalized racism" is being used interchangeably with the term "institutionalized discrimination." I am aware that the latter term is likely to be more acceptable to many educators but the reality is that in many countries such as Canada, Britain, West Germany, France and the United States (and many others), racism is alive and well in the educational system. The fact that racism is less commonly expressed in an overt way does not change the fact that it is still reflected in the priorities and policies of many schools. Lloyd Dunn's monograph, discussed in Chapters 3 and 7, shows how readily racist justifications of discriminatory schooling are forthcoming.

dominant middle-class culture. It is in these interactions that minority students are educationally disabled.

A concrete example will illustrate the subtle but potentially devastating ways that institutionalized racism can manifest itself in the well-intentioned interactions between educators and minority students. The following psychological assessment was one of more than 400 assessments of ESL students carried out in a western Canadian city (Cummins, 1984). It illustrates the assumptions that school psychologists and teachers frequently make about issues such as the appropriateness of standardized tests for minority students and the consequences of bilingualism for students' development.

Maria (not child's real name) was referred for psychological assessment by her grade 1 teacher, who noted that she had difficulty in all aspects of learning. She was given both speech and hearing and psychological assessments. The former assessment found that all structures and functions pertaining to speech were within normal limits and hearing was also normal. The findings were summarized as follows: "Maria comes from an Italian home where Italian is spoken mainly. However, language skills appeared to be within normal limits for English."

The psychologist's conclusions, however, were very different. On the Wechsler Preschool and Primary Scale of Intelligence (WPPSI), Maria obtained a Verbal IQ of 89 and a Performance IQ of 99. In other words, non-verbal abilities were virtually at the average level while verbal abilities were 11 points below the mean, a surprisingly good score given the clear cultural biases of the test and the fact that the child had been learning English in a school context for little more than a year. The report to Maria's teacher read as follows:

> Maria tended to be very slow to respond to questions, particularly if she were unsure of the answers. Her spoken English was a little hard to understand, which is probably due to poor English models at home (speech is within normal limits). Italian is spoken almost exclusively at home and this will be further complicated by the coming arrival of an aunt and grandmother from Italy.
>
> There is little doubt that Maria is a child of low average ability whose school progress is impeded by lack of practice in English. Encourage Maria's oral participation as much as possible, and try to involve her in extra-curricular activities where she will be with her English-speaking peers."

Despite the fact that the speech assessment revealed no deficiencies in Maria's spoken English, the psychologist has no hesitation ("There is little doubt..") in attributing Maria's academic problems to the use of Italian at home. The implicit message to the teacher (and parents) is clear: Maria's communication in L1 with parents and relatives detracts from her school performance, and the aim of the school program should be to expose Maria to as much L2 as possible in order to compensate for these deficient linguistic and cultural background experiences. In other words, the psychologist's assessment and recommendations reflect the assumptions of the "insufficient exposure" hypothesis (see Chapter 4).

How does this assessment (which was not atypical of the sample) represent institutional discrimination in action? First, the psychologist, despite being undoubtedly well-intentioned, lacks the knowledge base required to assess the child's academic potential. This is illustrated by the fact that an extremely culturally-biased test such as the verbal scale of the WPPSI is administered and an IQ score reported, by the failure to distinguish between conversational and academic aspects of L2 proficiency among ESL students, and by the assumption that use of L1 in the home is contributing to the child's academic difficulties. A large body of research shows that this is not the case (see Cummins, 1984).

Second, an implicit Anglo-conformity (assimilationist) orientation is evident in the lack of sensitivity to the fact that the child's cultural background and linguistic talents differ significantly from those upon whom the test was normed; the institutionalized racism is manifested not only in the lack of knowledge but in the total lack of awareness on the part of the psychologist (and presumably the institutions that trained her or him) that there are any knowledge gaps. The psychologist is not conscious that the child's culturally-specific experiences (in L1) might have any implications for the administration or interpretation of the test; there is also no hesitation in drawing inferences about the negative effects of L1 use in the home nor in making recommendations about language use in school despite the fact that the psychologist has likely had no training whatsoever on issues related to bilingualism.

In short, the institutional structure within which the psychological assessment takes place (e.g. with respect to policy/legal requirements and training/certification programs) orients the psychologist to locate the cause of the academic problem within the minority child herself. This has the effect of screening from critical scrutiny a variety of other possible contributors to the child's difficulty, e.g. the educational experiences to which the child has been exposed (see Coles, 1978). Because the psychologist is equipped only with psychoeducational assessment tools, the child's difficulty is assumed to be psychoeducational in nature. The psychologist's training has resulted in a tunnel vision that is out of focus with respect to the experiential realities of the children being assessed.

How do these subtle unintentional forms of institutional racism victimize minority children? As a result of the assessment, there is an increased likelihood that Maria will be reprimanded for any use of Italian with other Italian students in school, thereby promoting feelings of shame in her own cultural background. It is also probable that the child's parents will be advised to use English rather than Italian at home[3] If parents adhere to this advice, then they are likely not only to *really* expose the child to poor models of English, but also to reduce the quality and quantity of communication between adults and children in the home since they are likely to be much less comfortable in English than Italian. The importance of adult-child home interaction for future academic achievement has been demonstrated repeatedly (e.g. Wells, 1986) and thus, the advice to switch to English in the home has the potential to exert serious negative effects on children's development. Furthermore, it is likely to drive an emotional wedge between children and parents (including the recently arrived aunt and grandmother who will know no English) since parents may feel that communication of affection and warmth in Italian will reduce the child's future academic prospects.

Rodriguez (1982) provides an autobiographical account of the emotional schism brought about by teachers' advice to parents to switch from Spanish to English in the home:

> "One Saturday morning three nuns arrived at the house to talk to our parents ... I overheard one voice gently wondering, 'Do your children speak only Spanish at home, Mrs. Rodriguez?' ... With great tact the visitors continued, 'Is it possible for you and your husband to encourage your children to practice their English when they are at home?' Of course, my parents complied. What would they not do for their children's well-being? And how could they have questioned the Church's authority which those women represented? In an instant, they agreed to give up the language (the sounds) that had revealed and accentuated our family's closeness. The moment after the visitors left, the change

---

[3]This is still an extremely common practice in North American schools. For example, during the 1986-87 school year in Tornillo, Texas, a community composed overwhelmingly of Mexican-Americans, the school board sent home notices to parents requesting that they (the parents) punish their children when they were caught speaking Spanish at school. The board explained that it was necessary for parents to punish the children since teachers were prohibited by law from punishing children for speaking Spanish.

was obseved. '*Ahora*, speak to us *en ingles*', my father and mother united to tell us" (p. 20-21).

Rodriguez goes on to describe the effect of this language switch for the family's interaction at home:

> "The family's quiet was partly due to the fact that, as we children learned more and more English, we shared fewer and fewer words with our parents. Sentences needed to be spoken slowly when a child addressed his mother or father. (Often the parent wouldn't understand.) The child would need to repeat himself. (Still the parent misunderstood.) The young voice, frustrated, would end up saying, 'Never mind' - the subject was closed. Dinners would be noisy with the clinking of knives and forks against dishes" (p. 23).[4]

In summary, the example of Maria illustrates how students can become educationally disabled as a direct result of their interactions with well-intentioned educators. These interactions are mediated by the role definitions of educators which, in turn, are molded by a variety of influences; for example, the broader policy and legal structure within which educators operate, the institutional structure within which they have been trained, and the school and school district structures (e.g. principal-teacher, administrator-principal relationships) that determine priorities for action on a day-to-day basis.

Despite the appearance of change in North American education, these structures are essentially the same as the sociohistorical structures described in Chapter 2 which typically eradicated children's language and culture through overt violence (e.g. physical punishment for speaking L1). The violence has become covert - psychological rather than physical (see Skutnabb-Kangas, 1984). However, the message to minority children and communities is the same: to survive in this society your identity must be eradicated and your community must not threaten the power and privilege of the dominant group. With respect to the internalization of shame by parents and children, the results of this psychological violence may be even more devastating since the violence is covert and the institutionalized

---

[4]Rodriguez (1982) argues that this schism between children's lives in home and school, their private and public selves, is necessary and that bilingual programs are potentially detrimental to minority children because they create the illusion that it is possible for children to become fully integrated into American society without fully giving up their cultural identity. These arguments are examined in Chapter 7.

racism is hidden behind the genuine efforts of well-intentioned educators. These educators are themselves victims of the structure within which they operate since their professional goals of helping children succeed are frustrated by factors beyond their control and of which they are often unaware.

How can educators and communities collaborate to change the structure of institutionalized racism which makes school failure for a large proportion of minority children virtually inevitable? The first step is to recognize that minority students are failing academically, not primarily because of language differences, but because they are disempowered as a result of particular kinds of interactions with well-intentioned educators. When children's (or communities') identities become shrouded in shame, they lose the power to control their own lives in situations where they interact with members of the dominant group (e.g. classrooms). Consequently, they perform in school the way educators expect them to perform - poorly - thereby reinforcing educators' perception of them as deficient. Thus, for real change to occur, educational interventions must be oriented towards empowerment - towards allowing children to feel a sense of efficacy and control over what they are committed to doing in the classroom and in their lives outside the school. In other words, real change must challenge the power structure (i.e. the institutionalized racism) that disables minority children. The theoretical framework outlined below represents an intervention model based on this causal analysis of why and how minority children experience school failure.

A Theoretical Framework for Intervention

The framework presented in Figure 5-1 is adapted from Cummins (1986). As documented in Chapter 2, power and status relations between minority and majority groups appear to exert a major influence on school performance (Cummins, 1984; Ogbu, 1978). Minority groups that tend to experience academic difficulty (e.g. Finns in Sweden, Hispanic, Black, and Native American groups in the U.S., Franco-Ontarian, Black and Native groups in Canada) appear to have developed an insecurity and ambivalence about the value of their own cultural identity as a result of their interactions with the dominant group. Ogbu and Matute-Bianchi (1986) have provided a detailed review of the enormous variability in academic performance among linguistic minority groups. Among the phenomena they report is the fact that in Japan Buraku outcaste students (a very low status group) tend to perform poorly but when they immigrate to the United States they do as well as other Japanese students. The same phenomenon is noted with Japanese Koreans whose group originally went to Japan as colonial subjects in forced labor and who are regarded as very low status. In Japan, Koreans perform poorly in school but in the United States they perform relatively much better.

Another example noted in the Swedish and U.S. contexts is the fact that minority students from dominated groups who immigrate relatively late (about ten years of age) often appear to have better academic prospects than students of similar socioeconomic status born in the host country, despite much less exposure to the school language (Skutnabb-Kangas and Toukomaa, 1976). These findings have been attributed, in part at least, to the fact that these students have not experienced devaluation of their identity in the social institutions (e.g. schools) of the host country as has been the case for students born in that setting (see e.g. Cummins, 1984, 1986; and discussions in Epstein, 1977).

A central proposition of the theoretical framework is that minority students are disempowered educationally in very much the same way that their communities are disempowered by interactions with societal institutions. The converse of this is that minority students will succeed educationally to the extent that the patterns of interaction in school reverse those that prevail in the society at large. In short, minority students are "empowered" or "disabled" as a direct result of their interactions with educators in the schools. These interactions are mediated by the implicit or explicit role definitions that educators assume in relation to four institutional characteristics of schools. These characteristics reflect the extent to which:

1. minority students' language and culture are incorporated into the school program;

2. minority community participation is encouraged as an integral component of children's education;

3. the pedagogy promotes intrinsic motivation on the part of students to use language actively in order to generate their own knowledge; and

4. professionals involved in assessment become advocates for minority students by focusing primarily on the ways in which students' academic difficulty is a function of interactions within the school context rather than legitimizing the location of the "problem" within students.

Each dimension can be analyzed along a continuum, with one end reflecting an intercultural or anti-racist orientation (role definition) and

SOCIETAL CONTEXT

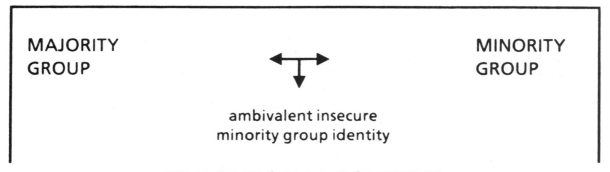

MAJORITY
GROUP

ambivalent insecure
minority group identity

MINORITY
GROUP

EDUCATIONAL CONTEXT

EDUCATOR ROLE DEFINITIONS

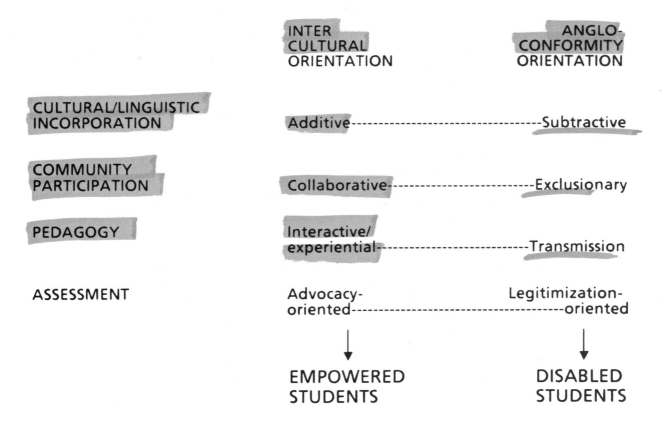

	INTER CULTURAL ORIENTATION	ANGLO-CONFORMITY ORIENTATION
CULTURAL/LINGUISTIC INCORPORATION	Additive------------------------------------Subtractive	
COMMUNITY PARTICIPATION	Collaborative-------------------------Exclusionary	
PEDAGOGY	Interactive/experiential---------------------------Transmission	
ASSESSMENT	Advocacy-oriented---------------------------------------Legitimization-oriented	

EMPOWERED
STUDENTS

DISABLED
STUDENTS

Figure 5-1 Empowerment of Minority Students: A Framework for Intervention

the other reflecting the more traditional Anglo-conformity (assimilationist) orientation. The overall hypothesis (prediction) is that this latter orientation will tend to result in the personal and/or academic disabling of minority students while anti-racist orientations (as operationally defined with respect to the framework) will result in minority student empowerment, a concept that, in the present context, implies the development of the ability, confidence and motivation to succeed academically.

1. Cultural/Linguistic Incorporation

Considerable research data suggest that for minority groups who experience disproportionate levels of academic failure, the extent to which students' language and culture are incorporated into the school program constitutes a significant predictor of academic success (see Chapter 4). In programs where minority students' L1 skills are strongly reinforced, their school success appears to reflect both the more solid cognitive/academic foundation developed through intensive L1 instruction and also the reinforcement of their cultural identity.

With respect to the incorporation of minority students' language and culture, educators' role definitions can be characterized along an "additive-subtractive" dimension (see Lambert, 1975, for a discussion of additive and subtractive bilingualism). Educators who see their role as adding a second language and cultural affiliation to students' repertoire are likely to empower students more than those who see their role as replacing or subtracting students' primary language and culture in the process of assimilating them to the dominant culture. In addition to the personal and future employment advantages of proficiency in two or more languages, there is considerable evidence that subtle educational advantages result from continued development of both languages among bilingual students. Enhanced metalinguistic development, for example, is frequently found in association with additive bilingualism (e.g. Diaz, 1986).

It is important to emphasize that schools can play a significant role in encouraging children to develop their L1 proficiency even in situations where bilingual education or heritage language teaching is not possible. Some of the ways in which schools can create a climate that is welcoming to minority parents and, at the same time, promotes children's pride in their linguistic talents have been noted by New Zealand educators (New Zealand Department of Education, 1988):[5]

---

[5] I am grateful to Jean Handscombe for bringing this excellent booklet to my attention.

- Reflect the various cultural groups in the school district by providing signs in the main office and elsewhere that welcome people in the different languages of the community;

- Encourage students to use their L1 around the school;

- Provide opportunites for students from the same ethnic group to communicate with one another in their L1 where possible (e.g. in cooperative learning groups on at least some occasions);

- Recruit people who can tutor students in their L1;

- Provide books written in the various languages in both classrooms and the school library;

- Incorporate greetings and information in the various languages in newsletters and other official school communications;

- Provide bilingual and/or multilingual signs;

- Display pictures and objects of the various cultures represented at the school;

- Create units of work that incorporate other languages in addition to the school language;

- Encourage students to write contributions in their L1 for school newspapers and magazines;

- Provide opportunities for students to study their L1 in elective subjects and/or in extracurricular clubs;

- Encourage parents to help in the classroom, library, playground, and in clubs;

- Invite second language learners to use their L1 during assemblies, prizegivings, and other official functions;

- Invite people from ethnic minority communities to act as resource people and to speak to students in both formal and informal settings.

2. Community Participation

It has been argued (Cummins, 1986) that minority students will be empowered in the school context to the extent that the communities themselves are empowered through their interactions with the school. When educators involve minority parents as partners in their children's education, parents appear to develop a sense of efficacy that communicates itself to children with positive academic consequences.

Although lip service is paid to community participation through Parent Advisory Committees (PAC) in many school programs, these committees are frequently manipulated through misinformation and intimidation (see Curtis, 1988). The result is that parents from dominated groups retain their powerless status, and their internalized inferiority is reinforced. Children's school failure can then be attributed to the combined effects of parental illiteracy and lack of interest in their children's education (for a recent example see Dunn, 1987, discussed in Chapters 3 and 7). In reality, most parents of minority children have high academic aspirations for their children and want to be involved in promoting their academic progress (Wong Fillmore, 1983). However, they often do not know how to help their children academically, and they are excluded from participation by the school.

Dramatic changes in children's school progress can be realized when educators take the initiative to change this exclusionary pattern to one of collaboration. For example, a two-year project carried out in an inner-city area of London (Haringey) showed major improvements in children's reading skills simply as a result of sending books home on a regular basis with the children for them to read to their parents, many of whom spoke little English and were illiterate in both English and their L1 (predominantly Bengali and Greek) (Tizard, Hewison & Schofield, 1982). The children in this "shared literacy" program made significantly greater progress in reading than a control group who received additional small-group reading instruction from a highly competent reading specialist. The differences in favor of the shared literacy program were most apparent among children who were initially having difficulty in learning to read. Both groups made greater progress than a third group who received no special treatment. Teachers involved in the home collaboration reported that children showed an increased interest in school learning and were better behaved (see also Topping, 1986; Topping & Wolfendale, 1985).

The teacher role definitions associated with community participation can be characterized along a *collaborative-exclusionary* dimension. Teachers operating at the collaborative end of the continuum actively encourage minority parents to participate in promoting their children's academic progress both in the home and through involvement in classroom activities. A collaborative orientation may require a willingness on the part of the teacher to work closely with mother tongue teachers or aides in order to communicate effectively and in a non-condescending way with minority parents.

Teachers with an exclusionary orientation, on the other hand, tend to regard teaching as *their* job and are likely to view collaboration with minority parents as either irrelevant or actually detrimental to children's progress. Often parents are viewed as part of the problem since they interact through L1 with their children at home. From the perspective of many teachers, parents' demands to have their languages taught within the school system further illustrates how misguided parents are with respect to what is educationally valuable for their children.

These attitudes reflect the ways in which teachers have defined their roles with respect to minority children and communities. They have accepted rather than challenged the power structure within which the education of minority students takes place. These attitudes, communicated subtly but surely to students, contribute directly to the disabling of minority students within the classroom.

3. Pedagogy

Several investigators have suggested that the learning difficulties of minority students are often pedagogically-induced in that children designated "at risk" frequently receive intensive instruction that confines them to a passive role and induces a form of "learned helplessness" (e.g. Beers & Beers, 1980; Coles, 1978; Cummins, 1984). Instruction that empowers students, on the other hand, will aim to liberate students from dependence on instruction in the sense of encouraging them to become active generators of their own knowledge.

Two major orientations can be distinguished with respect to pedagogy. These differ in the extent to which the teacher retains exclusive control over classroom interaction as opposed to sharing some of this control with students. The dominant instructional model in most western industrial societies has been termed a "transmission" (Barnes, 1976; Wells, 1982, 1986) or "banking" (Freire, 1973, 1983) model; this can be contrasted with an "interactive/experiential" model of pedagogy.

The basic premise of the transmission model is that the teacher's task is to impart knowledge or skills that s/he possesses to students who do not yet have these skills. This implies that the teacher initiates and controls the interaction, constantly orienting it towards the achievement of instructional objectives.

It has been argued that a transmission model of teaching contravenes central principles of language and literacy acquisition and that a model allowing for reciprocal interaction between teachers and students represents a more appropriate alternative (Cummins, 1984; Wells, 1986). This "interactive/experiential" model incorporates proposals about the relation between language and learning made by a variety of investigators, most notably, in recent years, in the Bullock Report (1975), and by Freire (1973), Barnes (1976), Lindfors (1980) and Wells (1986). Its applications with respect to the promotion of literacy conform closely to psycholinguistic approaches to reading (e.g. Goodman & Goodman, 1978; Smith, 1978) and to the recent emphasis on encouraging expressive writing from the earliest grades (e.g. Chomsky, 1981; Graves, 1983).

A central tenet of the interactive/experiential model is that "talking and writing are means to learning" (Bullock Report, 1975, p. 50). Its major characteristics in comparison to a transmission model are as follows:

- genuine dialogue between student and teacher in both oral and written modalities

- guidance and facilitation rather than control of student learning by the teacher

- encouragement of student-student talk in a collaborative learning context

- encouragement of meaningful language use by students rather than correctness of surface forms;

- conscious integration of language use and development with all curricular content rather than teaching language and other content as isolated subjects

- a focus on developing higher level cognitive skills rather than factual recall

- task presentation that generates intrinsic rather than extrinsic motivation

In short, pedagogical approaches that empower students encourage them to assume greater control over setting their own learning goals and to collaborate actively with each other in achieving these goals. The instruction is automatically "culture-fair" in that all students are actively involved in expressing, sharing, and amplifying their experience within the classroom. The approaches reflect what cognitive psychologists such as Piaget and Vygotsky have emphasized about children's learning for more than half a century. Learning is viewed as an active process that is enhanced through interaction. The stress on action (Piaget) and interaction (Vygotsky) contrasts with behavioristic pedagogical models that focus on passive and isolated reception of knowledge.

The relevance of these two pedagogical models for bilingual/multicultural education derives from the fact that a genuine multicultural orientation is impossible within a transmission model of pedagogy. To be sure, content about other cultural groups can be transmitted, but appreciation of other cultural groups can come about only through interaction where experiences are being shared. Transmission models exclude, and therefore, effectively suppress, students' experiences. Consequently, these teacher-centered approaches do not allow for validation of minority students' experiences in the classroom.

In this respect, transmission approaches operate in very much the same way as standardized tests. Minority students' experiences are systematically excluded from the curriculum and classroom just as items that might reflect culturally-specific experiences have no hope of making it into final versions of standardized IQ and achievement tests (see Cummins, 1984, for a description of how this discriminatory structure operates and is rationalized "scientifically").

4. Assessment

Historically, in many western countries, psychological assessment has served to legitimize the educational disabling of minority students by locating the academic "problem" within the student herself. This has had the effect of screening from critical scrutiny the subtractive nature of the school program, the exclusionary orientation of teachers towards minority communities, and transmission models of teaching that suppress students' experience and inhibit them from active participation in learning.

This process is virtually inevitable when the conceptual base for the assessment process is purely psychoeducational. If the psychologist's task (or role definition) is to discover the causes of a minority student's academic difficulties and the only tools at her disposal are psychological tests (in either L1 or L2), then it is hardly surprising that the child's difficulties are attributed to psychological dysfunctions. The myth of bilingual handicaps that still influences educational policy and practice was generated in exactly this way during the 1920's and 1930's.

Recent studies suggest that despite the appearance of change brought about by legislation such as Public Law 94-142, the underlying structure of the assessment process has remained essentially intact.   Mehan, Hertwerk and Meihls (1986), for example, report that psychologists continued to test children until they "found" the disability that could be invoked to "explain" the student's apparent academic difficulties.   Rueda and Mercer (1985) have also shown that designation of minority students as "learning disabled" as compared to "language impaired" was strongly influenced by whether a psychologist or a speech pathologist was on the placement committee.   In other words, with respect to students' actual behavior, the label was essentially arbitrary.   The Cummins (1984) study, discussed earlier, also revealed that although no diagnostic conclusions were logically possible in the majority of assessments, psychologists were most reluctant to admit this fact to teachers and parents.   With respect to overrepresentation of minority students in special education classes, the disabling structure has preserved itself simply by shifting the overrepresentation from classes for the retarded to classes for the learning disabled (Ortiz and Yates, 1983).

The alternative role definition that is required to reverse the "legitimizing" function of assessment can be termed an "advocacy" orientation.   The psychologist's or special educator's task must be to dismantle the traditional function of psychological assessment in the educational disabling of minority students; in other words, they must be prepared to become advocates for the child in scrutinizing critically the social and educational context within which the child has developed.   This implies that the conceptual basis for assessment should be broadened so that it goes beyond psychoeducational considerations to take account of the child's entire learning environment.   To challenge the disabling of minority students, the assessment must focus on the extent to which children's language and culture are incorporated within the school program, the extent to which educators collaborate with parents in a shared enterprise, and the extent to which children are encouraged to use language (both L1 and L2) actively within the classroom to amplify their experiences in interaction with other children and adults.   In other words, the primary focus should be on remediating the educational interactions that minority children experience.

It is worth noting that assessment and pedagogy are closely linked in that classroom teachers have considerable opportunities to observe children undertaking a variety of cognitive and academic tasks when the instruction is individualized and interactional.   This information can and should play an important role in assessment/placement decisions.   Within a transmission model, when the instructional tasks are teacher-imposed

rather than expressive of children's own experience, then the instruction tends to mirror the biases of standardized tests and consequently provides much less opportunity for observation of children's capacities.

In summary, an advocacy approach to assessment of minority children will involve locating the pathology within the societal power relations between dominant and dominated groups, in the reflection of these power relations between school and communities, and in the mental and cultural disabling of minority students that takes place in classrooms. These conditions are a more probable cause of the 300% overrepresentation of Texas Hispanic students in the learning disabled category than any intrinsic processing deficit unique to Hispanic children.

It should be emphasized that although the racism involved in the assessment process is structural, the actual discriminatory assessment itself is carried out by well-intentioned *individuals* who, rather than challenging a social and educational system that tends to disable minority students, have accepted a role definition and an educational structure that makes discriminatory assessment virtually inevitable. The implication is that although change processes may be initiated by external agents or factors, implementation of change can be successful only when it entails a role redefinition or change of "mind set" on the part of individual educators.[6]

Conclusion

This chapter has outlined a causal analysis of why minority students experience school failure and an intervention model that specifies directions for reversing this pattern of school failure. I have suggested that a pedagogy for empowerment requires educators to adopt

- an additive orientation to students' culture and language such

---

[6]In this regard, the change processes being implemented as part of the "educational reform" movement in the United States appear largely counter-productive. These processes are more likely to direct educators' role definitions towards interactions that disable minority students as a result of the fact that teachers themselves are being disempowered by means of pressure to continually increase students' standardized test scores. The change processes involved in "remediating" educational programs are unlikely to be successful if "reform" is transmitted from the top down to lower levels of the educational hierarchy, as has been the case in current American educational reform efforts. In this process everybody applies pressure on the level below and the motivation for change and/or learning is purely extrinsic. Children are unfortunate enough to be at the bottom of the educational hierarchy and thus they get drilled with skills and facts for regurgitation on tests so that teachers, principals, and other administrators can preserve their credibility (and jobs).

that students' L1 experiences can be shared rather than suppressed in the classroom;

- an openness to collaborate with community resource persons who can provide insight to students and educators about different cultural, religious, and linguistic traditions;

- a willingness to encourage active use of written and oral language so that students can develop their language and literacy skills in the process of sharing their experiences and insights with peers and adults; and

- an orientation to assessment in which the primary focus is on the interactions that students have experienced within the school system and on ways of remediating these interactions, where necessary.

Changes in these directions require, first, that educators become conscious of the disabling structure within which they are expected to operate (Freire's conscientization process); second, educators must decide if they are willing to challenge this structure; third, if educators are committed to empowering students, they must decide what forms their challenge to the power structure will take.

In promoting change, it is important for educators to be aware of the legal and policy status of minority education. They should forge links with other committed educators and community groups interested in promoting minority students' educational success and bring parents' legal rights to their attention. They should also patiently confront the misconceptions and contradictions of those opposed to bilingual education and inform them of the relevant research evidence. An invitation to sceptics to visit classrooms where empowerment bilingual education is being implemented can often demonstrate that what is involved is simply good education. In addition, pedagogical initiatives expressed in "mainstream" terms can often quietly undermine the institutionalized discrimination in schools. For example, initiatives related to creative writing, critical literacy, computer networks, parental involvement, and higher-order thinking skills conform to the rhetoric of many school systems and thus can slip by without appearing to challenge the power structure (see Shor, 1987, for many other examples). Even within the constraints of transitional bilingual programs, committed educators can often actively promote an additive orientation to children's language and culture while implementing these kinds of interactive/experiential teaching approaches. Some concrete examples of how the intervention model described above can be implemented are discussed in the next chapter.

CHAPTER 6

IMPLEMENTING CHANGE: CHALLENGING
THE DISABLING STRUCTURE

In the previous chapter, an intervention model was elaborated which outlined four dimensions along which changes in educators' role definitions are required in order to empower minority students. Concrete examples of ways in which this intervention model can be implemented are presented in this chapter. The following three illustrative interventions are discussed: first, the use of the "Descrubrimiento/Finding Out" math and science curriculum developed by Ed de Avila with both children and adults in the Passaic School District in New Jersey; second, the family literacy project conducted by Alma Flor Ada with parents, children and teachers in the Pajaro Valley School District in California; and third, the "Orillas" computer network project coordinated by Dennis Sayers in Connecticut and related networking projects being conducted in other parts of the country.

Each of these examples incorporates the first three dimensions highlighted in the intervention model, namely, an additive orientation to children's L1 development, community participation, and interactive/experiential pedagogy. Within the framework of interactive/experiential pedagogy, all three interventions apply the same approaches, with varying degrees of emphasis, namely, process writing, critical literacy, and cooperative learning. The interventions also implicitly embody particular images of students, teachers and the society their interactions in school will help form. These images are fundamentally different than those implied by the transmission approaches to pedagogy adopted in many current educational "reform" efforts in the United States.

In order to place the illustrative examples of empowerment pedagogy in context, current educational reform efforts in the United States will be briefly reviewed and the assumptions regarding students, teachers and our society implied in these reforms will be contrasted with those implied in empowerment pedagogy. Then, the related approaches of critical literacy, cooperative learning and process writing will be outlined, followed by a description of how these approaches were implemented in the three interventions.

Societal Images: Compliance versus Empowerment

The image of the learner implied by transmission approaches is of a consumer of pre-determined, pre-sequenced, and pre-digested knowledge. The learner has no input into what gets taught and it is assumed (e.g. by "direct instruction" approaches) that nothing worthwhile can be learned by students unless it has been explicitly taught by the teacher or some other adult. This assumption is patently false, as is clear from a moment's reflection on the vast amount of language (and other forms of knowledge) acquired through interaction by children prior to formal schooling.

Within transmission approaches, the teacher's job is to ensure that students can regurgitate appropriate facts and skills on demand. At first sight the teacher appears to be the active and controlling influence in the classroom. However, this is largely an illusion created by the passivity of the students. In reality, teachers are themselves being controlled and disempowered by higher levels of the educational hierarchy. They have little or no input into the content of the curriculum, nor into alternative means of achieving curricular objectives. In short, within a transmission approach the teacher's role is to drill skills into reluctant skulls. The image is more that of an assembly-line worker than of a critical, inquiring, creative developer of young minds (Cuban, 1984).

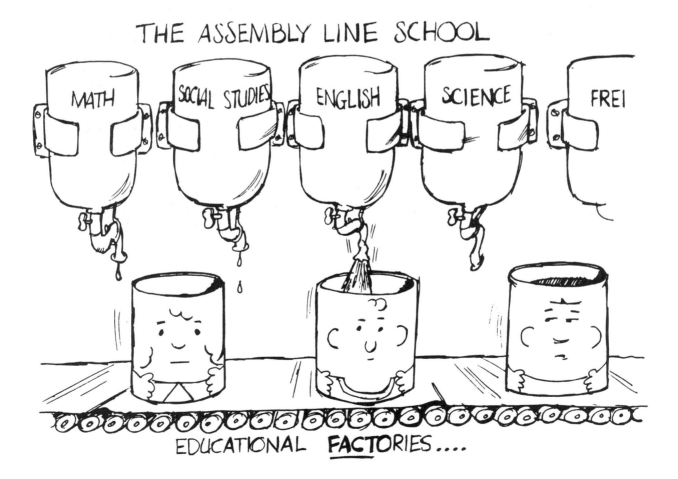

THE ASSEMBLY LINE SCHOOL

EDUCATIONAL **FACTORIES**....

These trends have been reinforced by current educational "reform" efforts in several States which emphasize behavioristic notions such as direct instruction, task analysis, time on task, mastery learning, lesson cycle, etc. The result has been an increased emphasis on ditto-sheet learning of isolated facts and skills. Since evaluation of teachers has become dependent on the extent to which they raise students' standardized test scores, there is no incentive for teachers to innovate, nor to encourage students' critical and creative thinking skills. Although lip-service is paid to these objectives, they are not reflected on the standardized tests and are therefore not reflected in the interactions that children experience in the classroom. Albert Shanker (1987), President of the American Federation of Teachers, has noted these trends with concern:

> "In response to this pressure teachers spend huge amounts of time drilling students in multiple choice questions and sample exams and teaching the strategies of test-taking. Wherever I go, I meet teachers who complain that they find it increasingly difficult to do real teaching. There's no time for concepts, for thinking, for stimulating discussions. All the time is spent on boosting test scores ... We may end up with a generation whose heads are full of little bits and scraps of knowledge and who are adept at picking from (a), (b), (c), or (d) but unable to write, express, think or persuade" (Education Week, January 14, 1987).

The image of our future society implied by this type of education is a society of compliant consumers who passively accept rather than critically analyze the forces that impinge on their lives.

The alternative image of the learner within an interactive/experiential model is of an explorer of meaning, a critical and creative thinker who has contributions to make both in the classroom and in the world beyond; students interpret and analyze facts rather than just ingest them. They read to learn rather than simply learn to read; they engage in creative writing both to collaboratively explore with teachers, parents and peers the horizons of their experience and to extend these horizons.

The teacher's role is to provide an environment where students can express, share and amplify their experience and to guide and facilitate this process. Teachers can promote empowerment and critical thinking skills only if they themselves are empowered and critical thinkers.[1]

---

[1] An excellent text outlining ways of integrating the learning of English both with students' lives outside the classroom and with teaching of other academic content is D. Scott Enright and Mary Lou McCloskey's *Integrating English: Developing English language and literacy in the multilingual classroom.* Reading, Mass: Addison-Wesley, 1988.

The society implied by this type of education is one where people have power, i.e. control over their own lives and the ability and confidence to make informed decisions about issues that affect their lives. The rhetoric of current educational reform in the United States proclaims these ideals but the classroom reality reeks of disempowerment, both of teachers and students.[2]

APPROACHES TO EMPOWERMENT PEDAGOGY

Critical Literacy

Ada (1986, 1988a and Ada and de Olave, 1986), on the basis of Freire's (1973) pedagogical approach, has outlined how critical thinking skills can be interwoven with a variety of curriculum content that involves reading. She distinguishes four phases in what she terms "the creative reading act":

1. **Descriptive Phase**. In this initial phase, children receive information. In other words, they learn what the text says. Appropriate questions at this level might be: Where, when, how, did it happen? Who did it? Why? These are the type of questions for which answers can be found in the text itself. Ada points out that these are the usual reading comprehension questions and that "a discussion that stays at this level suggests that reading is a passive, receptive, and in a sense, domesticating process" (1988a, p. 104).

2. **Personal Interpretative Phase**. After the information has been presented, children are encouraged to relate it to their own experiences and feelings. Questions that might be asked

---

[2]This perspective is essentially the same as that elaborated by Giroux and McLaren (1986) in their discussion of pedagogy for a democratic society and by other proponents (e.g. Shor [1987]) of critical pedagogy whose work has been influenced by Freire (1973). In criticizing transmission approaches to pedagogy, I do not intend to dispute the value of passing on the heritage of "Anglo-Western culture." On the contrary, I and many other educators would very much welcome students adopting a historian's perspective on "heritage" and "culture" by researching various sources and weighing alternative interpretations, including those of minority groups. For example, what interpretation might North American Indians have about the ways they have been traditionally depicted in historical texts that transmit "the heritage of Anglo-Western culture"? The value of transmitting information is certainly not at issue but what is at issue is the extent to which students and teachers should be encouraged to discuss alternative interpretations of the transmitted information. To deny teachers and students this right is to reduce teaching to indoctrination.

by the teacher at this phase are: Have you ever seen (felt, experienced) something like this? Have you ever wanted something similar? How did what you read make you feel? Did you like it? Did it make you happy? Frighten you? What about your family? Ada (1988a) points out that this process helps develop children's self-esteem by showing that their experiences and feelings are valued by the teacher and classmates. It also helps children understand that "true learning occurs only when the information received is analyzed in the light of one's own experiences and emotions" (p. 104).

3. **Critical Phase**. After children have compared and contrasted what is presented in the text with their personal experiences, they are ready to engage in a more abstract process of critically analyzing the issues or problems that are raised in the text. This process involves drawing inferences and exploring what generalizations can be made. Appropriate questions might be: Is it valid? Always? When? Does it benefit everyone alike? Are there any alternatives to this situation? Would people of different cultures (classes, genders) have acted differently? How? Why? Ada emphasizes that school children of all ages can engage in this type of critical process, although the analysis will always reflect children's experiences and level of maturity.

4. **Creative Phase**. This is a stage of translating the results of the previous phases into concrete action. The dialogue is oriented towards discovering what changes individuals can make to improve their lives or resolve the problem that has been presented. Let us suppose that students have been researching (in the local newspaper, in periodicals such as National Geographic, the Greenpeace magazine etc) problems relating to environmental pollution. After relating the issues to their own experience, critically analyzing causes and possible solutions, they might decide to write letters to congressional representatives, highlight the issue in their class/school newsletter in order to sensitize other students to the issue, write and circulate a petition in the neighborhood, etc.

The processes described by Ada (1988a) are very similar to those outlined by Freire (1973) and by Taba (1965) whose work still provides the framework for much curriculum development in the area of critical thinking in the North American context. As pointed out by Wallerstein

(1983, p. 197), however, Freire and Taba differ primarily in the final step of the process where Taba asks for summations and applications to other situations whereas Freire (and Ada) calls for action to promote alternatives to current problematic or negative situations. Also, curriculum development in the area of critical thinking based on Taba's work frequently treats it as just another time slot in the day rather than as part of a process that should be integral to *all* aspects of the curriculum. In other words, according to this view, critical thinking is regarded as a skill that should be transmitted in much the same way as other skills and facts.

Within an interactive/experiential pedagogical orientation, on the other hand, critical/creative thinking is manifested through active use of oral and written language for collaborative exploration of issues and resolution of the *real* problems that form the curriculum. In other words, the primary focus is on *process* rather than transmission of content. In an article entitled "Critical Literacy: Taking Control of Our Own Lives," Alex McLeod (1986) documents how a focus on complex issues such as racism, colonialism, and war led working-class students (in London, England) to explore the forces that affected their existence. He points out

> "Being literate in the 1980's means having the power to use language - writing and reading, speaking and listening - for our own purposes, as well as those that the institutions of our society require of us. The classroom processes by which that power is achieved include the first exercise of that power" (p. 37).

The content to which children's thinking and problem-solving is directed will stimulate active engagement ("time on task") only if it has direct relevance to children's lives (now or in the future). The daily newpaper is a better source of this type of content in subject areas such as science, social studies, and language arts than the sanitized facts that have been laid to rest in most textbooks and work-sheets.

Cooperative Learning

Cooperative learning refers to "the structuring of classrooms so that students work together in small cooperative teams" (Kagan, 1986, p. 231). Kagan (1986) has carried out a detailed review of the different cooperative learning methods and the large amount of research carried out on the consequences of cooperative learning for students' achievement, social development, and ethnic relations. The present outline relies heavily on Kagan's synthesis.

The context within which Kagan places the research on cooperative learning is the dominant trend in the United States towards classrooms and schools that "can be characterized as generally competitive, individualistic, and autocratic" (p. 238). Drawing on the conclusions of Goodlad's (1984) observations of more than one thousand classrooms, Kagan notes the fact that "remarkably, our society, which prides itself on democratic principles, has settled on autocratic models of teaching" (p. 239).

This is unfortunate in view of the data showing conclusively that cooperative learning techniques enhance academic achievement, and particularly so for minority students. Kagan reviews the meta-analysis of 46 studies carried out by Slavin (1983) which showed that

> "Of the 46 studies reviewed, 63 percent showed superior outcomes for cooperative learning; 33 percent showed no significant differences; and only 4 percent showed higher achievement for the control groups. Most importantly, however, a dramatic difference emerged among the studies as a function of cooperative learning method. Almost all studies (89 percent), which used group rewards based on individual achievement produced achievement gains" (Kagan, 1986, p. 244).

The achievement gains observed in cooperative classrooms are particularly dramatic for minority students. Whereas non-minority and high-achieveing students generally perform about as well in traditional and cooperative classrooms, low-achieving and minority students appear to be considerably more motivated to learn in cooperative classrooms. These conclusions are supported by studies conducted with low-status Arab students in Israel as well as with Black and Hispanic students in the United States.

Kagan concludes that

> "minority students may lack motivation to learn, but only when they are placed in traditional, competitive/individualistic classroom structures. As demonstrated so clearly by the ... [research], in a relatively short time what appears to be a long-term minority student deficiency in basic language skills can be overcome by transforming the social organization of the classroom. Thus, the gap in achievement between majority and minority students is best not attributed to personal deficiencies of minority students, but rather to the relatively exclusive reliance in public schools on competitive and individualistic

classroom structures" (p. 246-247).

Kagan argues convincingly that for a variety of reasons, related both to creation of a truly democratic society and promotion of educational equity, cooperative learning should be an integral part of the attainment of curriculum objectives in all subject areas. However, despite the overwhelming research evidence supporting cooperative learning, it is seldom mentioned in discussions of "effective schools" or current educational reform movements, which tend to stress teacher-controlled direct instruction approaches. Cooperative learning is easily integrated into language arts instruction that stresses process writing and critical literacy.

Process Writing

The extent to which writing activities had declined in North American schools was forcefully brought home to educators with the publication of Donald Graves' (1978) study entitled "Balance the Basics. Let Them Write." Graves documented the fact that writing received minimal attention in comparison to reading and most of the writing that students did carry out was copying. Feedback that students received on their writing tended to focus on the correctness of surface forms (e.g. grammar and spelling). This preoccupation with correctness of surface forms persisted despite considerable evidence that correction of students' writing errors and explicit teaching of grammar were not particularly effective. For example, Elley (1981) summarizes the findings of his extensive longitudinal study on the teaching of grammar as follows:

> "Pupils who had no formal grammar lessons for three years were writing just as clearly, fluently and correctly as those who had studied much grammar, the only apparent difference being that the pupils who hadn't studied grammar enjoyed English more ... The research evidence overwhelmingly shows that increasing the amount of analytic study of language has no positive effect on pupils' ability to read or write" (1981, p. 12).

Correction, in fact, can have negative consequences for writing development in much the same way as for spoken language acquisition. As expressed by Smith (1983):

> "Children do not learn from being corrected but from wanting to do things the right way. Most of the immense labor teachers put into correcting their students' work is wasted; it is ignored.

If it is not ignored, then it may have a negative effect, with children avoiding the words they fear they cannot spell or pronounce correctly. They do not become better spellers or speakers by writing or talking less. Correction is useful, and it is only paid serious attention to, when the student wants it and would indeed be offended if it were not given" (1983, p. 138).

In short, children acquire writing skills by engaging in writing activities that are creative and intrinsically interesting. Formal skills are gradually acquired in the context both of continued reading (Smith, 1982) and of projects to which children are actively committed. As Smith points out, children do not want "spelling mistakes in the poster they put on the wall, the story they are circulating, or the letter they will mail" (1983, p. 138). Rather than attempting to control this process, the teacher's roles include being a guide, facilitator, and most important, communication partner. Essentially, teachers organize the classroom in such a way that children's active involvement is maximized in projects to which the children themselves are committed.

Graves' (1983) work has begun to bring about a major change in the way writing is taught in North American schools. The change is esentially one from a transmission to an interactive/experiential model of pedagogy. The "process" approach which Graves has advocated emphasizes writing as a meaningful communicative activity in which there is a real purpose (e.g. publication of a book within the classroom), a genuine audience (e.g. peers, teachers, parents), and support systems to assist children work through the editing of successive drafts.

Although innovative within the North American context, these same ideas had been implemented by Celestin Freinet in France as early as the 1920's. Freinet's work resulted in a network of correspondence between schools in various regions of the country. Five thousand school newspapers and newsletters were published regularly, two of which, La Gerbe and Art Enfantin, became increasingly popular in several European countries (see e.g. Balesse and Freinet, 1973; Sayers, 1988).

The results of several projects with minority students suggest that the experience of creative writing is particularly significant in developing a sense of academic efficacy among these students (Brisk, 1985; Edelsky, 1981). Daiute (1985) has expressed the potential of interactionist approaches to writing in promoting this sense of efficacy:

"Children who learn early that writing is not simply an exercise gain a sense of power that gives them confidence to write - and write a lot. ... Beginning writers who are confident that they have something to say or that they can find out what they need to know can even overcome some limits of training or development. Writers who don't feel that what they say matters have an additional burden that no skills training can help them overcome" (p. 5-6).

Traditional approaches to writing that emphasize correctness of surface forms are particularly destructive for minority students whose knowledge of the school language in the early grades is frequently limited.

ILLUSTRATIVE EXAMPLES OF EMPOWERMENT PEDAGOGY

Descubrimiento/Finding Out in Passaic School District

Descubrimiento is a program for teaching math and science concepts that provides elementary school students the opportunity to work in small groups carrying out experiments and activities that illustrate the concepts being taught. Materials are made available in both English and Spanish and students are free to use either language. Students discuss the conduct of the experiment, what they observed and why particular phenomena occurred. Then they write up their results individually in workbooks which pose questions requiring both descriptions and explanations of the events. Thus, the program incorporates active use of oral and written language within the context of small group cooperation and critical inquiry.

Extensive evaluations of the program (see e.g. de Avila, Cohen, and Intili, 1981; and Cummins, 1984, for a summary) have shown it to be highly successful in developing not only math and science concepts but also language skills among minority students. In addition, it was found that the more students used language in the small-group settings and in their written reports, the more learning occurred. The results strongly support the Bullock Report (1975) principle that "talking and writing are means to learning."

The particular implementation of this program in the Passaic School District in New Jersey involved using the program as a vehicle to help parents learn English in addition to using it in the regular classroom. Parents were initially shown the program to familiarize them with what their children were doing in school but many expressed an interest in completing the program themselves (personal communication Ed de Avila, Francis X. Sutman, Cynthia Bilotta). Therefore training sessions for parents were implemented using similar procedures to those used with their children. This involved using the progam "to generate discussion,

curiosity, and interest so students will learn to find answers for
themselves" (Public Education Institute Quarterly, Spring, 1987, no. 4, p.
5). The results of the parent training were summarized as follows:

> "An informal survey of the parents found they all had enjoyed
> the program, and a majority thought the program would help
> their children. Four parents who participated in the program
> are now working as classroom assistants. 'We empowered
> parents too' said [Annette] Lopez [a teacher in the school
> system]" (Public Education Institute Quarterly Spring, 1987, no.
> 4, p. 5).

Among the reasons why initiatives such as this are likely to be successful
in promoting students' academic skills are the fact that they not only
involve parents with the school system but also promote interest and
familiarity among parents about what their children are doing in school
and stimulate discussion at home about their shared experience with the
program. This pattern is very evident in the next example.

The Pajaro Valley Family Literacy Experience

The Pajaro Valley School district serves a mostly rural population in the
area surrounding Watsonville, California. More than half the students in
the district are Hispanic and more than half of these drop out before
completing high school. This compares to 34.5% dropouts in the general
student population (Ada, 1988b). Since February 1986, a group of
Spanish-speaking parents varying in size between 60 and 100 have been
meeting once a month to dialogue (among themselves and with Alma Flor
Ada) about children's literature and to read stories and poems written both
by their children, and, increasingly, by themselves. Ada points out that
most of these parents have had very little schooling and many had never
read a book before much less thought about writing one.

Alma Flor Ada's involvement with the district arose out of an invitation
from the school librarian to participate in a "meet the author" program
during which she read some of her (Spanish) stories to the children and
discussed aspects of what is involved in the process of writing. Children's
enthusiasm was enormous and it was decided to follow up the interest that
had been stimulated in the children by involving their parents in a similar
creative literacy process.

The planning of the project (by Alma Flor Ada, Alfonso Anaya, director of
the bilingual program, and teachers) was carried out carefully in order to
encourage parental participation. For example, meetings were carried out

in the library rather than the school itself because of frequent negative associations that minority parents have with schools; the subject of the meetings was non-threatening, namely children's literature; parents were respectfully invited to participate (through written invitations in Spanish and follow-up personal phone calls); a parallel program for children was offered in a nearby room (films, storytelling, etc); and several teachers' aides offered to give rides to parents who lacked transportation. In addition, all the bilingual teachers participated in the meetings, which were conducted entirely in Spanish.

The initial discussion at the first meeting covered the purpose of the program and issues such as the importance of promoting children's first language proficiency and pride in their cultural heritage. In addition, parents' crucial role as their children's first and best teachers was stressed. According to Ada (1988b)

> "The results of this initial discussion were overwhelming. It was obvious that the parents were deeply moved. One mother stood up and explained: 'What is happening to us is that no one has ever told us that our children are worth something, and no one has ever told us that we are worth something' (p. 227).

The dialogue on these general themes was followed by a presentation of five children's story books, chosen primarily for their appeal in terms of literary content and presentation. Alma Flor Ada read each of the books aloud to the whole group of parents, dramatizing the action and showing the illustrations. Then parents were invited to select the book she or he wanted to take home and to join a small group for discussion of that particular book. These discussions were facilitated by the bilingual teachers who were careful to accept and validate everyone's participation while guiding the discussion to more reflective levels of analysis, following the general scheme outlined in Ada's (1988a) creative reading process described above.

In addition to a copy of the book he or she had chosen, each parent was given a list of questions organized according to the four phases of the creative reading process as a general guide for home discussions with their children, a list of suggested activities related to the book and a blank book in which children might be encouraged to write their own stories or dictate them for the parents to write.

From the second session, the parents have been meeting first in small groups according to which book they selected the previous month in order to talk about their experiences in discussing the books with their children. Then in a whole group format they read and listen to some of the stories the children have written or dictated. Finally, the new books are presented and small groups are formed to discuss them. All the sessions have been videotaped.

Ada sums up the major results of the program as follows:

> "parents have begun to read aloud to their children, the children have begun to bring home books from the school library, and parents and children have gone to the public library in search of books. At the first meeting we had a show of hands to find out how many parents had public library cards. None did. At a meeting nine months later almost everyone reported several visits to the library to check out books" (p. 223).

In addition, the teachers' aides have borrowed the videotapes and shown them in the community, thereby giving the children the opportunity of seeing their parents as characters on the television screen, reading aloud the stories created by the children. According to Ada, "the children have felt double pride, both in seeing their parents on the screen, and in hearing their own stories being read aloud." This has greatly increased children's motivation to write.

Other consequences are an increase in self-confidence and self-expression on the part of the parents, indicated by parents taking over the roles of small-group facilitators, giving presentations on the use of children's literature at the Regional Migrant Education Conference, and requesting the opportunity to purchase books in Spanish for their children, since the one book a month that they took home was insufficient. The parents also suggested compiling a book of the stories that their children have written, a project which has been carried out.

Ada quotes extensively from the parents themselves about their reaction to the program. Two examples will illustrate the empowerment process that took place over the course of these meetings:

> "Another mother said: 'Ever since I know I have no need to feel ashamed of speaking Spanish I have become strong. Now I feel I can speak with the teachers about my children's education and I can tell them I want my children to know Spanish. I have gained courage' ...

> One of the fathers said: 'I have discovered that my children can write. And I bring another story [written by his child]. But I have also discovered something personal. I have discovered that by reading books one can find out many things. Since my

children want me to read them the stories over and over again, I took them to the public library to look for more books. There I discovered books about our own culture. I borrowed them and I am reading, and now I am finding out things I never knew about our roots and what has happened to them and I have discovered that I can read in Spanish about the history of this country [the U.S.A.] and of other countries'" (1988, p. 235-236).

Although this project takes place entirely outside classrooms, the major components of the intervention model are very clearly present. An additive orientation to children's L1 is being promoted, the community is collaborating with the school in a shared enterprise, and the relationship between school staff and parents and between parents and children is based on genuine reciprocal interaction that encourages both the expression and amplification of experience.

The "Orillas" Project: Computer Networks and Empowerment

A significant innovation in recent years has been the use of the classroom microcomputer as a communications tool whereby students can carry out joint projects and exchange creative writing with students in distant locations. One of the pioneering efforts in exploring educational applications of computer networking was the *Computer Chronicles Newswire* (Mehan et al, 1984, 1986; Riel, 1985) which links students in San Diego with sister classes in Hawaii, Alaska, Mexico, and Japan. Applications of computer networking for minority students have been implemented by several investigators (e.g. Rosa and Moll, 1985; Sayers and Brown, 1987). The Rosa and Moll project, for example, linked Hispanic students in San Diego with native Spanish speakers in Madrid. The most extensive network focused on bilingual students in the United States is the *De Orilla a Orilla* - From Shore to Shore - project coordinated by Dennis Sayers in Connecticut (see Sayers, 1986a, 1986b, 1988; Sayers and Brown, 1987).

A major focus of the "Orillas" project has been the promotion of English and mother-tongue (Spanish) literacy through the sharing of elementary school children's writings in both languages. Children in Puerto Rico, Connecticut, San Diego, and Tijuana (Mexico) have communicated with "sister classes" virtually on a daily basis, reporting on issues that directly concern their lives. In addition to computer-mediated communication, videotapes made by the children have also been exchanged. Sayers (1986a) expresses the transformation of students' (and teachers') classroom roles within the project:

"In a sense, students in the *Orillas* classes are learning how to write by role-playing: they are "reporters" when they research and write local news stories; they are "editors" when they critique articles or select news from the many articles that come over the newswire; they even become "correspondents" whenever they send their stories to their colleagues overseas.   Yet in another more important sense, these language learners are not playing at all, for when their paper comes out, all the quotation marks around their "roles" disappear. They really *are* reporters, editors, and correspondents" (1986a, p. 8).

The three approaches to empowerment pedagogy highlighted above, namely, critical literacy, cooperative learning, and process writing, are clearly integrated into the activities that arise in classrooms that participate in a computer network.   Research carried out on computer networking shows that children write considerably more than previously and their enthusiasm for writing increases dramatically (Mehan et al, 1986).   For minority students, the utility of their first language becomes obvious through its use for communication with native speakers of the language in the country of origin.   The computer has acted as a catalyst for interactive/experiential learning that puts the inner city in contact with the global village and minority children in touch with their cultural roots.

Investigators involved with computer networking among minority students have also begun to explore community participation in the process. Specifically, Estaban Diaz and Luis Moll in San Diego and Pedro Pedraza in New York have established after-school settings for parents and children to get together to use computers and apply them to tackling issues in their lives.   For example, in the New York project, it has been found that the computers have been an important motivating force in helping adults overcome their fear of reading and writing in both Spanish and English.   A Macintosh laboratory donated to the project by the Apple Corporation will be used by the community for popular education projects and to produce income and publications for the community.   The project has been incorporated so that total control rests with the community.

The goals of these projects are both to empower the community itself and to take advantage of the intellectual and cultural resources within the community for promoting the academic development of children.   The experience to date has been that these after-school settings help in the process of giving children and their communities a voice to express, share and reinforce the validity of their experience.[3]

CONCLUSION

The theoretical model outlined in Chapter 5 analyzed minority students' academic failure or success as a function of the extent to which schools reflect or counteract the power relations that exist within the broader society. Specifically, language minority students' educational progress is strongly influenced by the extent to which individual educators become advocates for the promotion of students' linguistic talents, actively encourage community participation in developing students' academic and cultural resources, and implement pedagogical approaches that succeed in liberating students from instructional dependence. The interventions that have been reviewed in this chapter illustrate how students, educators and communities can be empowered when the individual role definitions of educators and the institutional role definitions of schools are redefined to challenge the underlying disabling structure.

This analysis suggests a major reason for the relative lack of success of previous attempts at eradicating the educational underachievement of minority students during the past 20 years. The individual role definitions of educators and the institutional role definitions of schools have remained largely unchanged despite "new and improved" programs and policies. These programs and policies, despite their cost, have simply added a new veneer to the outward facade of the structure that disables minority students. The lip service paid to initial L1 instruction, community involvement, and nondiscriminatory assessment, together with the more recent emphasis on "effective schools" have succeeded primarily in deflecting attention away from the attitudes and orientation of educators who interact on a daily basis with minority students. It is in these interactions that students are either disabled or empowered. In the absence of individual and collective educator role redefinitions, schools will continue to reproduce, in these interactions, the power relations that characterize the wider society and make minority students' academic failure virtually inevitable.

To educators genuinely concerned about alleviating the educational difficulties of minority students, this conclusion may appear overly bleak. I believe, however, that it is realistic and optimistic, as directions for

---

[3]The information regarding these projects is derived from presentations made at the conference on "Collaborative Writing Across Cultures" organized by the New England Multifunctional Resource Centres (March, 1987).

change are clearly indicated rather than obscured by the overlay of costly
reforms that leave the underlying structure essentially intact. Given the
societal commitment to maintaining the dominant/dominated power
relations, we can predict that educational changes threatening this
structure will be fiercely resisted. This is in fact the case for each of the
four structural dimensions of the intervention model.[4]

A major way in which institutions resist change is to rationalize the
disempowerment of minority children and communities as being in their
own best interests. The process is the same as that which has occurred
historically (see Table 2-1) where the school failure of minority children
and the societal failure of their parents were attributed to intrinsic
deficiencies. In order to help children the school had to eradicate these
deficiencies; hence, the assault on children's language and culture and the
consequent internalization of shame by the victims.

Academic researchers played an important role in this process by
"proving scientifically" that minority children's failure was due to factors
such as bilingualism, cultural deprivation, genetic inferiority etc (see
Hakuta, 1986). They legitimized the violence against children in schools
and helped to obscure contradictions between the rhetoric of equality and
the reality of domination.

In a similar way, it is necessary today for those who wish to maintain the
status quo to demonstrate the inferiority of empowerment pedagogy in
comparison to programs that reflect and reinforce the societal power
structure. Academics contribute to this process primarily by two means:
first by defining the framework of discourse to exclude the real alternatives
so that empowerment pedagogy is not even discussed; and second, through
a campaign of disinformation designed to deflect attention away from
research findings that might challenge the disabling structure. These
processes are considered in the next chapter.

---

[4]Although for pedagogy the resistence to sharing control with students goes beyond
majority/minority group relations, the same elements are present. If the curriculum is not
predetermined and presequenced, and the students are generating their own knowledge in a
critical and creative way, then the reproduction of the societal structure cannot be
guaranteed - hence the reluctance to create truly independent learners and to liberate
students from instructional dependence.

CHAPTER 7

DISINFORMATION IN THE INFORMATION AGE: THE ACADEMIC CRITICS OF BILINGUAL EDUCATION

The term "disinformation" refers to the systematic spreading of false information in order to confuse and disorient the opposition. Although the term is usually associated with the activities of groups such as the CIA and KGB, the phenomenon of disinformation is no less evident in debates on domestic political issues such as the education of minority students. For example, proponents of efforts to make English the official language of the United States have consistently argued that bilingual education hinders children's acquisition of English and other academic skills, despite the overwhelming research evidence that this is not the case.

For present purposes, we can distinguish two broad types of disinformation: first, the deliberate spreading of false information for political ends where those who are spreading the information know that the information is false; the second, and in the bilingual education situation, more common type of disinformation is where the false information is genuinely believed by those spreading it. This second phenomenon merits the pejorative term "disinformation" in cases where there is no excuse for being ignorant and/or misinformed since the relevant information is readily available. Those in positions of power and influence (e.g. media commentators, politicians, academics) have an ethical responsibility both to inform themselves of the relevant research and to attempt to be logical and rational in the way they interpret this research.

This second type of disinformation involves not so much a conscious "conspiracy" as a selective inattention to awkward facts and questions. Thus, in the 1920's and 1930's, researchers were very quick to attribute differences they observed between minority bilingual and majority monolingual children to the debilitating effects of bilingualism, despite the fact that so many obvious variables were confounded with bilingualism (e.g. socioeconomic status, language of testing, violence against minority children in schools, etc). They also did not consider the obvious question of why bilingualism appeared to exert no adverse effects on children of the rich and powerful. In short, the process involved abdicating logic and the scientific method in order to screen out potential explanations that might compete with the preconceived and societally-approved explanation; in other words, the explanation that contributed to the preservation of the societal power structure.

The same type of disinformation process appears to be operating today with respect to the effects of bilingual education. The data on bilingual education is both clear and abundant, yet the myth has been perpetuated that there is little data and what there is is worthless. Similarly, opponents of bilingual education have steadfastedly refused to ask any question that would challenge the "insufficient exposure" assumption and their advocacy of English-only immersion. The screening out involved in maintaining this "double-think" process is quite awesome in view of the fact that an enormous amount of research data, including virtually every evaluation of every bilingual program that has ever been evaluated anywhere in the world, quite clearly refutes the insufficient exposure assumption. In no case is there a linear relationship between exposure to the majority language and achievement in that language, and in many cases, as noted in previous chapters, there is an inverse relationship.

For opponents of bilingual education to acknowledge this overwhelmingly consistent pattern in the research data would entail asking how we can explain it and what the policy implications are. This would lead to the interdependence principle and the fact that minority children's L1 proficiency can be promoted at no cost to English achievement. This conceptual process has not been pursued because to do so would effectively eliminate the psychoeducational legitimization for eradicating minority children's language and culture. The rhetoric of equality could no longer be invoked to obscure the reality of domination.[1]

In this chapter, I review the process of disinformation practised by academics opposed to bilingual education. A cavalier attitude towards research evidence that is inconsistent with belief systems is perhaps not too surprising in the political arena. However, our expectations for academics are somewhat different since their training has focused explicitly on how to interpret and evaluate empirical evidence. Thus, it is appropriate to consider the evidence against bilingual education that has been invoked by academic critics. The purpose of this is two-fold: first to consider the validity of alternative interpretations of the research evidence that has been reviewed in Chapters 3 and 4; and second, to explore the broader issues of why highly respected academics make recommendations affecting the lives of millions of children that are absolutely devoid of both

---

[1] As in most politically-charged debates, both types of disinformation have probably been practised by proponents and opponents of bilingual education. Proponents have certainly not been anxious to point to the inadequacy of the linguistic mismatch assumption. I can remember, for example, discussing a workshop I was about to give on bilingual education with one of the conference organizers and saying that I thought it important for people to realize that the usual rationale for bilingual education, namely, the linguistic mismatch hypothesis, was oversimplified and could not adequately account for the research data. The organizer suggested that it wasn't a good idea to bring that up since it might just confuse people.

empirical evidence and logical coherence.

A first observation in reviewing the academic literature on bilingual education is that the vast bulk of this literature in both the United States and internationally is supportive of the educational merits of bilingual programs for both majority and minority students. Within the United States, despite the largely negative media coverage of bilingual programs, there are only a few academics who have argued against the educational validity of bilingual education. Most of the arguments reduce to the following: there is minimal evidence that bilingual education is effective in comparison to alternative programs, and English-only immersion programs represent a more promising alternative supported empirically by the results of Canadian immersion research.

This line of argument was first articulated by Noel Epstein (1977) but its elaboration into a coherent position was carried out by Keith Baker and Adriana de Kanter (1981) in their detailed review of research evidence on bilingual education. Much of the initial scepticism regarding the effectiveness of bilingual education derived from the findings of the American Institutes for Research (AIR) report (Danoff et al, 1977, 1978) that transitional bilingual programs appeared to be no more effective than English-only programs in promoting academic development among minority students. Claims of empirical support for English immersion programs have been made by Russell Gersten and John Woodward (1985a, 1985b). A monograph by Lloyd Dunn (1987), an article by Nathan Glazer (Glazer and Cummins, 1986), and printed comments by both Diane Ravitch and Herbert Walberg (General Accounting Office, 1987) have all supported English immersion over bilingual education. Finally, Richard Rodriguez' (1982) influential autobiographical novel "Hunger of Memory" articulates a unique perspective in opposing bilingual education and other forms of affirmative action. The Epstein, AIR, and Baker and de Kanter reports have all been treated in detail elsewhere and thus will be only briefly reviewed here. The more recent contributions will be discussed in greater detail.

Early Critiques: Epstein and the AIR Report

The first serious educational challenges to the rationale for bilingual education came in 1977 with the publication of Noel Epstein's monograph "Language, Ethnicity and the Schools" and the AIR study on the impact of ESEA Title VII Spanish/English bilingual programs (Danoff et al, 1977, 1978). Epstein pointed out that research evidence in support of bilingual education was meagre and also that the rationale for bilingual education was by no means as clearcut as advocates suggested. The success of

French immersion programs in Canada, he argued, showed that "the language factor itself can neither account for nor solve the educational difficulties of these minority students" (1977, p. 59).

As is clear from previous chapters, Epstein's questioning of the "linguistic mismatch" rationale for bilingual education is clearly valid and appropriate. However, his report fails to adopt a theoretical perspective in that it does not consider the assumptions underlying alternative positions. Had he done this he would have seen that there is abundant evidence refuting the "insufficient exposure" assumptions which he implicitly endorses in advocating experimentation with English immersion programs. Epstein also fails to consider the major differences in sociocultural context between French immersion programs in Canada and the situation of minority students in the United States. However, as an initial critical inquiry into the relation betwen policy and research in the area of bilingual education, Epstein's monograph represents an intelligent, if flawed, critique. It raised important questions and challenged bilingual educators to clarify the rationale for bilingual education, which was not as self-evident as many had assumed.

Suspicions that the "real" purpose of bilingual education had more to do with promoting cultural pluralism and language maintenance received a boost when the AIR study reported that, according to teacher judgements, less than one-third of the students enrolled in bilingual classrooms were there because of their need for English instruction (although both Title VII [bilingual program] and non-Title VII Hispanic students were functioning at approximately the 20th percentile on measures of English academic functioning). In addition, the results of comparative analyses showed that students in Title VII programs were doing no better academically than non-English background students in regular programs.

The AIR study has been criticized by numerous researchers (e.g. Gray, 1977; O'Malley, 1978; Swain, 1979). The major criticisms are that:

1. Data from effective and ineffective programs were aggregated with the result that negative results from programs experiencing serious implementation difficulties as a result of factors such as bilingual teacher unavailability, curriculum inadequacy, district lack of support, etc, would have obscured any positive impact of high quality bilingual programs. For example, only half of the Title VII teachers in the study were proficient in English and Spanish, and only 26% had bilingual teaching credentials.

2. Related to this was the fact that the Title VII and non-Title VII treatments were not clearly separated in that many of the non-Title VII teachers and aides were bilingual (while many of the Title VII staff were not) and some of the students in non-Title VII programs had received bilingual education, although for a shorter period of time, on average, than Title VII students. These students may have been exited from bilingual programs on the basis of their English proficiency, which further confounds the comparison since these students are likely to be better language learners than those who were retained in the bilingual program. The treatments were defined on the basis of funding rather than instructional content and thus no inferences can be made about the impact of bilingual education since there are no data on the extent to which "bilingual education" was going on in the Title VII classrooms.

In short, the AIR study tells us nothing about the effects of bilingual education, except to point to large variation in the quality and outcomes of all programs for Hispanic students.

The Baker and de Kanter Report

A detailed review of the literature on "The Effectiveness of Bilingual Education" was undertaken by two staff members of the Office of Planning, Budget and Evaluation in the U.S. Department of Education and published in 1981. The major conclusions of this literature review were as follows:

- "Schools *can* improve the achievement level of language-minority children through special programs.

- The case for the effectiveness of transitional bilingual education is so weak that exclusive reliance on this instructional method is clearly not justified ... Therefore ... each school district should decide what type of special program is most appropriate for its own setting.

- There is no justification for assuming that it is necessary to teach nonlanguage subjects in the child's native tongue in order for the language-minority child to make satisfactory progress in school ...

- Immersion programs, which involve structured curriculums in English for both language and nonlanguage subject areas, show promising results and should be given more attention in program development (de Kanter and Baker, Education Times, October 5, 1981.

There have been many critiques and rebuttals of the Baker/de Kanter report both from independent agencies and from agencies of the U.S. Government (e.g. National Institute of Education, Office of Civil Rights). It is sufficient to quote the conclusions of the American Psychological Association (1982) to indicate that the report has been largely rejected by researchers, despite its major impact in legitimizing the Reagan administration's policy in regard to bilingual programs.

"The Department of Education draft report entitled "Effectiveness of Bilingual Education: A Review of the Literature" does NOT (emphasis original) support the conclusion that bilingual education is ineffective, inappropriate, or unnecessary. In fact, it does not even attempt to address such questions. In debates on bilingual education in which the issues are defined in such terms, the study can be ignored - because it is irrelevant ...

The scientific quality of the report is questionable. Inconsistencies are apparent in the application of the methodological standards utilized. The evaluation question adddressed by the study was limited, and an arbitrary and narrow definition of 'acceptable data' was utilized" (pp. 8-9).

Similar sentiments are expressed in other critiques of the report (e.g. Willig, 1981/82).

Much of the difficulty in interpreting the Baker/de Kanter literature review derives from their categorization of vastly different forms of bilingual education as "transitional bilingual education" (TBE). In fact, the "structured English immersion" program in McAllen Texas that Baker and de Kanter describe as "promising" involved more L1-medium (Spanish) instruction (about 50-60 minutes a day) than a large number of so-called transitional bilingual programs in the United States. As Willig (1981-82) points out, the program director of this program considered it a bilingual program.

A tendency to play games with labels is also evident in Baker and de Kanter's review of Legaretta's (1979) evaluation of a 50/50 Spanish-English morning/afternoon program. Baker and de Kanter acknowledge that this is one of the best designed research studies that they reviewed but suggest that the success of the program is more appropriately attributed to the fact that it is "an alternate immersion program" (1981, p. 15). In extrapolating from the Canadian immersion data, they also fail to emphasize that L1 instruction is regarded by Canadian researchers and educators as a crucial component of immersion programs and that these programs are varieties of bilingual education, taught by bilingual teachers, and designed to promote full bilingualism.

The most serious problem with the Baker/de Kanter review is the total lack of any coherent theoretical orientation in the report. They implicitly assume that the theory of bilingual education predicts a linear incremental pattern of gains in English achievement as a function of the program. To the extent that there has been any widely accepted "theory" of bilingual education, it has tended to predict that students will approach grade norms only near the end of elementary school as transfer of academic skills from the conceptual foundation that has been established in L1 begins to bear fruit. In other words, gains will be cumulative but not necessarily incremental in a linear way (see e.g. Troike, 1978). Thus, failure to find a positive effect on English achievement at the grade 1 level in a program where relatively little instruction has been through L1 can in no sense be interpreted as a negative finding. Yet this is the assumption underlying Baker and de Kanter's interpretation of the research evidence.

It is interesting that Willig's (1985) meta-analysis of essentially the same data as Baker and de Kanter (quoted in Chapter 4) reached a very different conclusion supportive of bilingual education. Also, virtually all the evaluation results reviewed in the Baker and de Kanter report are entirely consistent with the interdependence principle (discussed in Chapter 4) in that minority students instructed through a minority language (L1) for all or part of the school day performed at least as well academically in the majority language (English) as equivalent students who were instructed totally in the majority language. In short, it is ironic to note that these data refute the implicit "insufficient exposure" hypothesis upon which Baker and de Kanter base their call for "structured immersion."

A final point worth noting with respect to the Baker and de Kanter report is the way in which they defined the framework of discourse as "transitional bilingual education versus structured immersion." Many North American researchers of bilingual programs (particularly those involved in evaluations of the Canadian French immersion programs, e.g. Wallace Lambert, Richard Tucker, Merrill Swain, Margaret Bruck, Fred Genessee, and myself) have been extremely critical of "quick-exit" transitional bilingual programs, regarding them as very much inferior to "enrichment" or "two-way" bilingual programs in which schools would promote an additive bilingualism among both majority and minority students together (see Genesee, 1985, 1987a, 1987b). Yet because of the irresponsible aggregation of very different programs under misleading labels, there is no way to argue for these enrichment alternatives within the context of the debate defined by the Baker/de Kanter report. Thus, in arguing against the conclusions of the Baker/de Kanter report, advocates of enrichment bilingual education found themselves defending an emasculated program (quick-exit TBE) of which they were highly critical.

What function do reports such as the Baker/de Kanter report serve within the context of societies attempting to preserve dominant-dominated power relations? The process over the past decade appears to have been to pay lip-service to the rhetoric of educational equity by funding various forms of compensatory programs while ensuring that potentially empowering pedagogical programs (i.e. those that potentially challenge institutional racism in schools, e.g. two-way bilingual programs) do not qualify for funding. Thus, the intervention goals are defined narrowly in terms of learning English and, as far as possible, only programs that pose little threat to the power structure get implemented (namely, emasculated quick-exit transitional programs). However, since it has transpired that even these programs have affected the power structure in providing jobs for Hispanics and other minorities (even though for the most part they have not reversed minority students' school failure), it is regarded as desirable to eliminate them; this becomes an urgent priority in view of the changing demographics which potentially pose a real threat within a democratic country. Thus, the next step must be to demonstrate that these programs (not surprisingly) do not work very well and should therefore be eliminated in order to help minority children succeed academically. Thus, the status quo (submersion under the label of "structured immersion") can be reinstated while preserving the myth that minority students' needs are being met. This point is elaborated in the final chapter.

Gersten and Woodward: A Case for Structured Immersion

Gersten and Woodward (1985a) claim to have found empirical evidence that structured immersion that uses the "direct instruction model" (i.e. DISTAR) produces large academic gains among minority students. Their initial discussion of the rationale for immersion programs reveals a truly incredible ignorance of the Canadian research upon which they base their arguments. For example, they note the fact that Baker and de Kanter "called public attention to the promising research findings from Canada on *structured immersion* (emphasis original). With structured immersion, all instruction is done in the commonly used language of the school (English in the U.S., French in Canada).

... Difficult new words are pretaught, sometimes using the child's native language.

... Santiago, in the March 2, 1983, <u>Education</u> <u>Week</u>, said that 'the immersion method has only been tried with middle class children.' His statement is not accurate; the bulk of the Canadian research was with low-income students" (1985, p. 75-76).

There has been a vast amount of research on French immersion programs in Canada and this research has been reported extensively in many academic jounrnals and books. It is therefore astonishing to see statements such as those above. First, in French immersion programs, children's L1 (English) is usually introduced about grade 2 or 3 and its use increased as children go up the grades so that by grade 5 about half the instructional time is spent through English. Thus to say that all instruction is done in French is totally inaccurate.

Second, French immersion programs are based explicitly on the premise that language is acquired through *use* not through explicit instruction out of the context of meaningful communication. Vocabulary is virtually never pretaught, any more than it is in the process of children acquiring their first language.

Third, although researchers have argued that French immersion programs are appropriate for low-income students and should not be restricted only to middle-class children (e.g. Genesee, 1987a, Cummins, 1984; Swain and Lapkin, 1982), the vast majority of children in French immersion programs come from middle-class backgrounds and very little research data are available on the performance of working-class children in these programs. Gersten and Woodward (1985b) reiterate their claim that Canadian immersion programs involved predominantly working-class students in their response to Santiago's (1985) rebuttal of their original article, stating that

"there were four studies other than the St. Lambert study, all of which involved children from working-class families. The results of structured immersion with these students were comparable to those found with the middle-class children in the

St. Lambert study" (1985b, p. 83).

Gersten and Woodward seem to believe that only five studies of French immersion have been carried out in Canada, and four of these involved working-class students. In fact, Swain and Lapkin's (1982) bibliography in their book on immersion contains more than 500 citations, most of these empirical studies, and that number has probably doubled since 1982.

How convincing is the empirical data presented by Gersten and Woodward? They describe results of two programs that used DISTAR with minority students, one group of Hispanic origin near the Mexican Border in Texas (Uvalde), and the other predominantly of Asian origin in California (Pacific City). In the Uvalde evaluation no comparison group was available and thus the evaluation data would be dismissed according to the criteria set up by Baker and de Kanter (see Santiago, 1985). When tested at the end of grade 3, after three years of DISTAR, the children were reported to be performing close to national norms on the language (i.e. usage, tense, punctuation, etc) and math subtests of the Metropolitan Achievement Test. However, scores on the reading subtest were considerably lower, at the 34th percentile, just slightly above the median district score in previous years (30th percentile).

Gersten (1985) reports longitudinal data from the Pacific City program that suggests better progress in English in the early grades for minority students in a DISTAR-based immersion program than for students in a transitional bilingual program. However, the numbers of students involved in this evaluation were extremely small; the first cohort involved only 12 immersion program students and nine bilingual program students while the second involved only 16 and seven in each group. These numbers scarcely constitute an adequate sample upon which to base national educational policy, especially since DISTAR-type drills are likely to be much more similar to standardized test content than the program to which the comparison group was exposed.

There is little question that DISTAR can effectively drill children in low-level mechanical skills such as decoding and computation. However, performance on literacy tasks that involve comprehension tends to be much lower. For example, Becker (1977) reports a progressive decline in reading comprehension scores of DISTAR students between grades 1 and 6, sliding from the 70th to about the 30th percentile. The results are similar to those reported by Gersten and Woodward. In other words, on the major component of English language proficiency required to get information from texts (e.g. in Social Studies, Science, etc.) as well as succeed in English langue arts, DISTAR shows no positive effects for minority students (a detailed critique of research on DISTAR is presented in

Cummins, 1984).

This is in contrast to the data emerging from adequately conceptualized (i.e. late-exit) bilingual programs which show performance close to grade level by the end of elementary school (for reviews see California State Department of Education, 1985; Cummins, 1981b, 1984; Krashen and Biber, 1987; Troike, 1978). Gersten and Woodward (1985b) end their response to Santiago with the question "Where's the data?" noting that "we fail to see any empirical evidence of bilingual students taught in Spanish ever catching up after a seven-year period" (p. 84). As with their "analysis" of immersion programs, they haven't looked very hard to find data that might contradict their preconceptions.

It is interesting that Gersten and Woodward call attention to the large-scale longitudinal comparison of structured immersion and bilingual programs then being initiated by David Ramirez of SRA Technologies. As noted in Chapter 4, the initial findings of this study show an inverse relation between exposure to English and achievement in English, with immersion students performing at a considerably lower level in English than students in both quick-exit and late-exit bilingual programs (see Education Week, 1986, April 23, p. 1 and 10).[2]

A final point in relation to the Gersten and Woodward article concerns their reduction of the framework of discourse to "structured immersion versus transitional bilingual education," as in the Baker de Kanter report. For example, in reviewing Lambert's injunction against immersion for minority students, they note that

> "He claims that typical compensatory education models will not work. The only salvation is transitional bilingual education, involving introduction of a 'separate English language instructional component when it is certain that the child's home language has taken root and it is a secure base for starting the buildup of English, a stage that may not be reached until a child enters the 2nd or 3rd grade'" (Gersten and Woodward, 1985, p. 76).

To anybody familiar with bilingual education research and policy, it is

---

[2]It is interesting to note that Keith Baker is the Education Department's program officer monitoring this study and the initial results, according to James Crawford in Education Week (1986, p. 10) have led him to slightly modify his views to favor including more L1 instruction in structured immersion because of the "fatigue" the learner might experience from instruction totally through English.

clear that what Lambert is discussing is a "reverse immersion" or two-way bilingual program where minority children are "immersed" in their L1. The goal is additive bilingualism involving high levels of both English and L1 literacy.   To label this type of program as "transitional bilingual education" is a travesty of what Lambert has eloquently argued for on many occasions (e.g. Lambert, 1975) which is directly opposed to the monolingual monocultural goals of transitional bilingual education. However, when the issues are conceptualized within this framework, true empowerment of minority students does not become a policy option for open discussion.

Glazer: Stirring the Melting Pot

Nathan Glazer's views on bilingual education were outlined in a journal called "*Equity and Choice* which asked both him and me to respond to a series of questions on bilingual education (Glazer and Cummins, 1985). While admitting a role for "taking cognizance of native language, using it for part of the school day [and] continuing it after transition to English for purposes of maintaining facility," he expresses concern that some bilingual programs are "keeping children in classes conducted primarily in their native language as long as possible (p. 47).

In response to a question on the best methodology for teaching English as a second language, Glazer responded as follows:

> "I don't think (probably) there is one 'best' way. But all our experience shows that the most extended and steady exposure to the spoken language is the best way of learning any language" (1985, p. 48).

Glazer here abdicates his academic (and ethical) responsibility to examine and rationally interpret the research evidence rather than remaining at the level of assumption and "common sense." As noted earlier (Chapter 4), the data overwhelmingly support the fact that there is no direct relationship between amount of exposure to English and development of English academic skills among minority students, obviously given a certain minimum amount of exposure to English.

Glazer's answer to the the subsequent question regarding how long it takes for children to achieve sufficient proficiency in English for them to be able to learn school subjects successfully through English instruction similarly reveals a total ignorance of the research. This, however, did not stop him from articulating his opinion:

"How long? It depends. But one year of intensive immersion seems to be enough to permit most children to transfer to English-language classes" (p. 48).

As discussed in Chapter 3, the data, in fact, show that on the average it takes at least 4-5 years for ESL students to attain grade-appropriate levels in English cognitive/academic skills (Collier, 1987, 1988; Cummins, 1981c; Wong Fillmore, 1983), although conversational skills may become fluent considerably sooner.

The point I wish to make here is that even those posing as "experts" in the field appear to have little hesitation in making pronouncements regarding bilingual education that are totally at variance with the research data but are consistent with their sociopolitical concerns; in Glazer's case, as with many other commentators, these sociopolitical concerns relate to the dangers of creating a separate Hispanic enclave in American society (1985, p. 51). Regardless of the legitimacy or otherwise of these concerns, the reality is that they are spreading disinformation by avoiding abundant opportunities to inform themselves about what the research on bilingual children's development is actually saying.

The same appears to be true for two other commentators whose views are briefly noted in a recent General Accounting Office (GAO) report on bilingual education.

Ravitch and Walberg: The General Accounting Office Report

The procedure followed by the GAO involved assembling a group of ten "experts" in the area of bilingual education and asking them to respond to questions in regard to the extent to which the Department of Education's policy directions were consistent with the research evidence. Secretary Bennett, for example, called bilingual education "the same failed path on which we have been travelling" and suggested that the current law is "a bankrupt course" the result of which is that "too many children have failed to become fluent in English" (GAO Report, 1986, p. 4). The overall conclusions of the ten experts are summarized as follows:

"The experts' views on the official statements we asked them to review indicate that the department interpreted the research differently in several major ways. First, only 2 of the 10 experts agree with the department that there is insufficient evidence to support the law's requirement of the use of native language to the extent necessary to reach the objective of learning English. Second, 7 of the 10 believe that the department is incorrect in characterizing the evidence as showing the promise of teaching methods that do not use native languages. Few agree with the department's suggestions that long-term school problems experienced by Hispanic youths are associated with native-language instruction. Few agree with the department's general interpretation that evidence in this field is too ambiguous to permit conclusions" (1987, p. 3).

Letters from two of the experts, Herbert Walberg of the University of Illinois at Chicago and Diane Ravitch of Teacher's College, New York, dissenting from the conclusions of the GAO Report are attached to the report as an Appendix. Both are highly respected academics, Walberg in the field of educational evaluation and Ravitch in history of education. As might be predicted from the sceptical (but extremely lucid) review of the evolution of bilingual education policy contained in her book "The Troubled Crusade: American Education 1945-1980" (Ravitch, 1983), Ravitch fails to see any strong evidence for bilingual education in the literature reviewed:

"I was one of the minority who saw very clearly in the material you circulated the repeated statement that the research available is too weak, too inconclusive, and too politicized to serve as a basis for national policy. The paucity of the available research was noted in several of the articles you sent us. If the majority of the panel chose to ignore this, I must say that I am not much impressed by the majority's vote" (GAO, 1987, p. 73).

Based on research carried out on second language acquisition in foreign countries and in the U.S. military, Walberg expresses himself more strongly in favor of a total immersion approach "for teaching English and getting non-English-speaking students into the mainstream of American life." Because much recent research on bilingual education is "wretchedly planned and executed," Walberg prefers to

"place more weight on earlier research carried out before the single approach [transitional bilingual education] was pressed, and research carried out in foreign countries and by the U.S. military. In my opinion, this research which was not prominent in the selection of reviews GAO supplied to us, shows the superiority of large amounts of high intensity exposure for learning a second language, which a gigantic amount of research on learning in general also supports" (GAO, 1987, p. 72).

There are several obvious, albeit understandable, misconceptions in

Walberg's position. First, he interprets the issue as being one of second language learning despite the fact that a vast amount of research shows that linguistic factors (e.g. insufficient exposure to English, home-school language switch) cannot account for the research data and that academic rather than conversational skills in English are involved in minority children's school failure. Second, none of the research he refers to as supporting his position involves bilingual education; for example, the U.S. military research involves adults, whose first language is well-established, learning a second language through high intensity exposure. This research, in fact, supports the interdependence principle, in showing that the better developed students' English academic skills (their language aptitude) the more proficiently they learn additional languages. If Walberg (and Ravitch) had examined the research data carefully they would have seen that the Baker and de Kanter review, as well as others, show clearly that there is either no relationship or a negative relationship between amount of exposure to English for minority students in elementary schools and their academic achievement in English. To reiterate, ALL the research data on bilingual programs, international and U.S., show this consistent pattern and yet so-called "experts," refuse to acknowledge, let alone try to account for, these data. WHY?

It is interesting also to note that at the time when the Walberg and Ravitch letters were written (September 1986), the initial results of the study funded by the Education Department comparing immersion with bilingual education had been available for about six months (Education Week, April 23 , 1986) and had been widely discussed. An ethical question is why these results (of a well-controlled large-scale study supervised by a proponent of English immersion [Keith Baker]) were not even mentioned by Walberg and Ravitch. What appears to be happening is that for those who feel a strong sociopolitical commitment against bilingual education (or cultural pluralism or other associated constructs), common sense arguments regarding the obvious superiority of intensive exposure to English in school tend to become immune from critical scrutiny and incompatible evidence is either ignored or dismissed. This pattern emerges very clearly in Lloyd Dunn's critique of bilingual education.

Dunn: "Teachers are not Miracle Workers"

Some of Dunn's (1987) naive and patronising views on the genetic inferiority of Hispanics and their lack of effort on behalf of their children have been discussed in Chapter 3. Here we are concerned with his views on bilingual education and his proposal for immersion programs "with supplemental services" as the most appropriate policy option for Puerto Rican and Mexican-American students. Since these students suffer from a "lack of intellectual, scholastic, and language aptitude ... it is clear that these children are not, as a group, able to cope with the confusion of two languages in the regular grades" (p. 76). Dunn does acknowledge the research data "on the need to develop proficiency in one's native language before undertaking English as a second language" (p. 73) and thus suggests that some minority children might not be ready for English immersion until they are beyond 6 years of age. However, his main thrust is to argue against L1 promotion on the grounds that "20 years of experimentation with so-called 'bilingual education' has not worked well, and will not, even with further tinkering, and therefore ... it is time to abandon this movement in favor of alternate procedures that are likely to be more effective" (p. 66).

What evidence does Dunn cite to dismiss bilingual education in favor of English immersion? He refers to the AIR (1977) and Baker and de Kanter (1981) reports as indicating lack of impact of bilingual education. Dunn notes Willig's (1981-82) documentation of "serious problems" with these two reports but argues that "it seems safe to conclude that their conclusion is sound" (p. 70). He suggests that the conclusion of these reports should come as no surprise since "the scholastic ability of most Puerto Rican and Mexican-American children is too limited to succeed well in two languages and to handle switching from one to the other efficiently" (p. 70). The only "evidence" presented for English immersion as an alternative is his own experience in teaching immigrant students in Western Canada in the 1930's.

To his credit, Dunn does acknowledge the existence of what he terms the Spanish Bilingual-Bicultural Maintenance Approach. This is the type of enrichment bilingual program recommended unanimously for minority students by researchers who have evaluated French immersion programs in Canada. Sometimes termed "reverse immersion," it involves "immersing" minority students in their L1 in the early grades in order to develop a strong conceptual foundation that will provide a basis for acquiring academic skills in English. The amount of English instruction gradually increases to around 50%-60% by the end of elementary school, much as is the case with French immersion programs. It is desirable for English-background students also to be participants in these immersion programs as a means of developing additive bilingual skills. The available research suggests that these reverse immersion or two-way bilingual programs are highly successful for both minority and majority students (see Cummins, 1984; Genesee, 1987a, 1987b). Dunn, however, is either unaware of, or choses to ignore this research. He dismisses these programs as follows:

"Under the 'maintenance theory' (or excuse), in extreme cases, some Mexican-American pupils are taught almost exclusively in Spanish by Mexican-American activist teachers, who repeatedly point out to the pupils that they are an oppressed group, and therefore obligated to assist in social change. With this focus, it is not surprising that these childern are not prepared to switch over to English at the end of elementary school, and have not adequately mastered the regular elementary school subject matter" (p. 67).

All the evidence that I am familiar with regarding this type of program in the United States and in Canada among minority francophone students (see Cummins, 1983, 1984) indicates exactly the opposite to what Dunn claims (without reference to any empirical evidence).

Dunn's claims regarding bilingual education are almost tragi-comic. For one who dismisses opponents of his favored views on test bias (it does not exist) as manifesting largely an "emotional and irrational defense reaction" (p. 62) and those who oppose English immersion as showing "irrational extremism" (p. 71), Dunn's total failure to consider the research data on bilingual education is staggering.

Once again, the question arises as to why the actual data on bilingual education has been screened from any kind of rational consideration. Dunn obviously has access to the research and theory, since my book (Cummins, 1984) and other works on bilingual education are cited (e.g. McLaughlin, 1984). Yet the arguments appear not to have penetrated.

Richard Rodriguez: Hunger of Memory

Of the various academic rejections of bilingual education presented in this chapter, the only position for which I have any respect is that presented by Richard Rodriguez (1982, 1985). In contrast to the disinformation rationalized in pseudo-scientific terms offered by most of the academic critics considered above, Rodriguez makes no claim to scientific validity for his views. He bases his opposition not on any form of empirical evidence or scientific logic but on a logic woven from the pain of his own experience. The trauma of passing from the private world of warm sounds to the cold public world of English was discussed briefly in Chapter 5. Rodriguez' argument against bilingual education is that it holds out a romantic but unrealistic promise of an easier passage from private to public worlds, a passage that would not entail sacrificing the intimacy and warmth of the private for the cold utility and necessity of the public.

Applying cold scientific criteria to this argument, it is clear that there is no evidence to support the position advocated by Rodriguez. The enormous legacy of school failure among Hispanic children illustrates just how difficult is the passage from private to public about which he speaks so eloquently. Extrapolation from his own ($N = 1$) successful emergence from the trauma of early schooling to generalized statements about program alternatives clearly has no scientific credibility, especially in view of the huge numbers of Hispanic children who have failed educationally under similar conditions. Also, the growing evidence that validating rather than eradicating children's cultural identity in the sphere of public institutions can reverse this pattern of school failure cannot lightly be dismissed.

I find Rodriguez' account valuable, however, because of the insights he provides (probably inadvertantly) about the psychology of dominant-dominated relationships within American society. Some of these insights summarized in an essay on bilingual education published in the New York Times (November 10, 1985, p. 83) are worth quoting in detail:

"The official drone over bilingual eduction is conducted by educationists with numbers and charts. Because bilingual education was never simply a matter of pedagogy, it is too much to expect educators to resolve the matter. Proclamations concerning bilingual education are weighted at bottom with Hispanic political grievances and, too, with middle-class romanticism.

... in private, Hispanics argue with me about bilingual education and every time it comes down to memory. Everyone remembers going to that grammar school where students were slapped for speaking Spanish. Childhood memory is offered as parable; the memory is meant to compress the gringo's long history of offenses against Spanish, Hispanic culture, Hispanics. ... Bilingualism becomes a way of exacting from gringos a grudging admission of contrition - for the 19th century theft of the Southwest, the relegation of Spanish to a foreign tongue, the injustic of history. ...

The child's difficulty [in language acquisition] will turn out to be psychological more than linguistic because what he gives up are symbols of home. I was that child! I faced the stranger's English with pain and guilt and fear. Baptized to English in school, at first I felt myself drowning - the ugly sounds forced down my throat - until slowly, slowly ... suddenly the conviction took: English was my language to use.

> Bilingual enthusiasts bespeak an easier world. They seek a linguistic solution to a social dilemma. They seem to want to believe that there is an easier way for the child to balance private and public, in order to believe that there is some easy way for themselves. ... The debate is going to continue. The bilingual establishment is now inside the door. Jobs are at stake. Politicians can only count heads; growing numbers of Hispanics will insure the compliance of politicians.
>
> Publically we will continue the fiction. We will solemnly address the issue as an educational question, a matter of pedagogy. But privately, Hispanics will still seek from bilingual education an admission from the gringo that Spanish has value and presence. Hispanics of middle class will continue to seek the romantic assurance of separateness. Experts will argue. Dark-eyed children will sit in the classroom. Mute" (1985, p. 63).

What I find interesting about this is Rodriguez' painfully clear depiction of the price exacted for participation in mainstream institutions: namely the eradication of children's first language and culture and the internalization of shame. Rodriguez also correctly, I believe (see Chapters 2 and 5), identifies the central issues as sociopolitical, rather than educational in a narrow sense. He describes the desire of Hispanics to reverse the historical pattern of subjugation, and their use of bilingual education as a wedge to attain this goal. The resistence to allowing Hispanics "inside the door" on the part of the dominant group is also clearly implied in Rodriguez' account. In short, he appears to provide an experiential account of dominant-dominated power relationships and their consequences for children in the early years of schooling that fits closely with that offered, from a very different perspective, in the present analysis.

Where my perspective differs from Rodriguez' is that I believe that Hispanics' use both of bilingual education and constitutional provisions for educational equity as a wedge to get "inside the door" is an appropriate and useful strategy, whereas he appears to question it, almost in a fatalistic way, on the grounds that the power structure is so well entrenched that it is a romantic dream to believe that the private and public worlds can be productively merged without destruction of the private.

Also, unlike Rodriguez (apparently), I also believe that there is a role for empirical evidence in discussions of educational policy. Thus, I find convincing evidence (including Rodriguez' own biographical account) that the mute Hispanic child is considerably more likely to be found in English-only or structured immersion classes ("drowning - the ugly sounds forced down my throat") than in classes where the child's language and culture are validated, classes to which the parents have access, and where children's experiences are amplified through collaborative exploration.

Conclusion

I have tried to show that the academic critics of bilingual education have operated at a level of scientific inquiry that is extremely superficial (with the exception of Rodriguez who has no interest in empirical evidence). They have either ignored the research evidence or considered it only in terms of questions that *logically* cannot be answered. For example, the central question of whether bilingual education is effective assumes that "bilingual education" can reasonably be thought of as one phenomenon and also that we have a clear understanding of what "effectiveness" implies.

Neither of these conditions is met, and hence the issues become mystified with the result that it becomes easy to claim that the research evidence is mixed or insufficient for policy. For example, it is clear that there are a large variety of bilingual education program models, and, within models, pedagogical practices and student populations vary enormously. Thus, to aggregate all this variation under the rubric "transitional bilingual education" with no theory for disentangling the effects of program variation is to ensure that there will be so much noise in the data that virtually no conclusions regarding "effectiveness" will be possible.

The problem is compounded by the absence of any theory in most of the evaluations and reviews regarding the meaning of "effectiveness," specifically the expectations or predictions regarding what different types of bilingual program should achieve and how long it should take to do it. For example, if the theory or expectation (implicit or explicit) of how a bilingual program should work dictates that students should be capable of transferring to an English-only program within a year, then a bilingual program that does not achieve this goal is ineffective. On the other hand, the theory might specify that it can take most of the elementary school years for minority students to deepen their academic knowledge of both L1 and English in order to transfer successfully to an all-English program. Within the context of this theoretical prediction, the "effectiveness" of transitional bilingual programs could not be adequately assessed until students had completed most of their elementary schooling in the program.

Related to the process of aggregating data from very different programs and framing the questions in terms of undefined notions of "effectiveness" is the elimination from the framework of discourse of any options other than "transitional bilingual education" and "structured immersion." This appears to provide policy-makers and educators with a clear choice of options but in reality what this reduction of options does is eliminate from consideration any programs that might genuinely empower minority children and communities.

Academics, despite their training in methods of scientific inquiry, have collaborated in this process of disinformation. In fact, they have internalized the disinformation such that their own belief systems are not disturbed by awkward questions and facts. How else can one account for the failure among academics and researchers to ask why it is that minority students taught through the medium of their L1 for a significant proportion of their early schooling do not suffer any loss in the development of English academic skills? In other words, why is exposure to English in school either not related or inversly related to achievement in English among minority students? The burying of this question cannot be explained by ignorance of the data. Virtually all the evaluations reviewed by Baker and de Kanter (1981) show this pattern.

In view of the overwhelming evidence against the "insufficient exposure" assumption and the access of academics who promote English-only immersion to this evidence, it is legitimate to inquire why they have failed to question this assumption and what function their silence serves.

Although spurious, arguments about the self-evident validity of intensive exposure to English for minority students have served to emasculate many bilingual programs, leading to the implementation of relatively ineffective "quick-exit" models rather than the considerably more effective programs aimed at biliteracy. And because such quick-exit programs usually do not require or encourage any personal or institutional redefinitions on the part of educators, institutionalized racism in the schools is preserved. In fact, it is probably preserved even more effectively because there is the appearance of change to meet "the needs" of minority students. The hysterical/paranoid reaction that even these minimal changes evoke from groups such as "U.S. English" reinforces the illusion that real educational change has occurred.

As Rodriguez (1985) notes from a different perspective, to the extent that typical "transitional bilingual education" programs have brought about any real change, it has been less in the sphere of promoting educational equality than in letting Hispanics (and other minorities) "inside the door" and promoting a consciousness among minorities of issues related to equity and power. The issue of bilingual education has become symbolic of past injustice and current institutionalized racism.

Within this context, the psychoeducational concerns of policy-makers, educators and academics about bilingual education hindering the acquisition of English simply mask the more valid concern that bilingual education programs have increased the status and power of the Hispanic minority at a time when demographic changes are already posing a threat to the dominance of the Anglo majority in several parts of the country. This threat of bilingual education to the societal power structure is examined in the last chapter.

CHAPTER 8

"AGAINST AMERICAN CONCEPTS": BILINGUAL
EDUCATION - SUBVERSIVE OR PATRIOTIC?

The major theme that has emerged from press commentary on bilingual education during the past 15 years is the fear that bilingual education will subvert the social stability of the United States and threaten "our way of life" (Cummins, 1981a). Commentators frequently point to societies, particularly Canada, where bilingualism appears to be associated with divisiveness and separatist tendencies and warn that similar fragmentation is being encouraged in the United States by means of federal promotion of bilingual education. As noted in Chapter 2, Bethell (1979) described this trend to restore the United States to "its component ethnic parts" as "a death wish" on the part of the federal government, while President Reagan in 1981 suggested that a bilingual education program openly and admittedly dedicated to preserving students' native language was "absolutely wrong and against American concepts".[1]

Among the "American concepts" presumably intended by President Reagan was the traditional commitment to freedom and equality of opportunity that has been honored at a rhetorical level since the birth of the constitution, but only taken seriously at a legal/institutional level during the past 20 years. The historical data reviewed in Chapter 2 (and the vast amount of documentation related to the civil rights of Black and other minority students) demonstrates that traditional "American concepts," as implemented educationally, have been openly dedicated to *segregating* Black, Hispanic and Indian students from mainstream schools. The reality has been (and still is) that most students from these minority groups are educated to a level where they qualify only for menial jobs, thereby reproducing the low social status of the group across generations.

The fear that has engendered such a negative reaction to bilingual

---

[1]The invocation of Quebec as an example of bilingual education leading to separatist tendencies is ironic in view of the fact that there is considerably *less* bilingual education in Quebec than in most other parts of Canada. Separatist tendencies in Quebec arose as a result of economic domination within the province by the small English-background minority (about ten percent). The successful challenge to this domination by the Parti Quebecois government dissipated all desire to separate on the part of the Quebec people and the separatist movement is currently dead; ironically, the Parti Quebecois, which championed both the movement and the elevation of the status of French, is out of office. The Quebec experience strongly suggests that empowerment of previously dominated groups dissipates separatist tendencies whereas continued domination and discrimination promotes such tendencies. The repression of Spanish advocated by the "U.S. English" organization is much more likely to raise Hispanic consciousness of discrimination and promote divisiveness rather than the opposite.

education is the fear of social change, of minority empowerment. James Reston in an article entitled "Habla espanol? Not in our schools" (Journal, Milwaukee, Wisconsin, February 5, 1981) points out that "in many states, the Hispanic population has grown to the point where it may not only influence but hold the decisive margin in state and local elections." He goes on to comment on the problems of ever increasing Hispanic illegal immigration and to praise the Reagan administration's withdrawal of regulations that would have solidified the institutionalization of bilingual education as "a first step" in dealing with these myriad Hispanic problems. In a similar vein, Dunn (1987), as already noted, refers to minority children "taught almost exclusively in Spanish by Mexican-American activist teachers, who repeatedly point out to the pupils that they are an oppressed group, and therefore obligated to assist in social change" (p. 67).

More recently, John Tanton, Chairman of U.S. English, provided a rare glimpse of the social concerns underlying the crusade against bilingual education. As summarized by *Education Week*:

> "The document, which was unrelated to the organization's business, warned that Hispanics and other ethnic groups with high birthrates could pose a threat to whites. It also suggested that the growing numbers of Catholic Hispanic immigrants might affect American principles of church-state separation. The memo - and other reports that a contributor had endorsed forced sterilization in countries with high population growth - prompted the resignations of Linda Chavez, the group's president, and Walter Cronkite, the former CBS News anchorman, who served on the organization's board" (November 2, 1988, p. 12).

Linda Chavez characterized Mr. Tanton's statements about Hispanics and other ethnic groups as "repugnant" (Education Week, October 26, 1988, p. 4).

The fear and insecurity evident in the rhetoric directed at the "internal threat" of bilingual education (i.e. minority empowerment) is strikingly similar to the paranoia engendered in the Reagan administration by the overthrow of the Somoza regime by the Sandinistas in Nicaragua. I shall argue in this chapter that the similarities are more than superficial; in fact, the overriding goals of the dominant group are virtually identical in both situations, namely, to reverse a sociopolitical change that they perceive as threatening their ability to control and exploit a traditionally dominated group.   The   processes   through   which   information   is manipulated to promote domestic acceptance of this goal are also very similar; in both cases, empirical realities that contradict the rhetoric are denied or dismissed, a process that is supported by the media, and blatent logical inconsistencies in the policies are ignored.

The purpose of pursuing this analysis is to place the bilingual education debate into a broader context of power relations between rich and poor groups (or nations) so that the nature of the debate can be better understood by proponents of empowerment pedagogy for minority students. Many advocates for minority students still view the opposition as essentially well-intentioned but misinformed. They view their major task as informing them about the empirical evidence for bilingual education so that rational decisions can then be made on the basis of this research evidence. While some of those opposed to bilingual education are genuinely well-intentioned and will be swayed by empirical evidence supporting bilingual programs, a considerably larger proportion (as evidenced by media comment) are more concerned with the threat that bilingual education represents to the societal power structure ("American concepts"). This component of the dominant group will continue to vehemently reject educational empowerment of minority students. In fact, the more empirical evidence is produced that certain types of programs result in personal and academic growth among minority students, the more vehement will be the denial of this evidence and the rejection of these programs by the dominant group. Thus, the reality is the opposite to that assumed by many proponents of bilingual education who believe that positive results of bilingual programs will increase the likelihood of these programs being accepted and implemented more extensively. This process of invalidating "the threat of a good example" (Chomsky, 1987a) is illuminated very clearly in the Nicaraguan debate.[2]

It is important to restate here that, *at one level*, the United States has committed itself since the mid-sixties to educational equity more vigorously than perhaps any other nation. A large amount of funds has been expended on research to try to understand the nature of minority underachievement and on intervention aimed at reversing

---

[2]The analysis in this Chapter draws on Noam Chomsky's extensive analyses of U.S. foreign policy during the past 20 years. Chomsky is universally acknowledged as the world's most prominent linguist and his work has revolutionized the field; however, within the United States his political writings are virtually unknown. This may appear surprising given their highly controversial nature and the sheer quantity of writing Chomsky has undertaken in this area (more than 15 books since the late sixties). Chomsky (1987b) notes that his books on contemporary issues are generally reviewed quite widely in Canada, England, Australia and elsewhere but only sporadically in the United States. While his books are totally banned in the Soviet Union, the same effect is achieved within the United States by means of the media and major publishers simply ignoring their existence.

underachievement. This major public commitment has been matched by the enormous dedication of many educators who go way beyond their job descriptions in the extent to which they attempt to promote academic and personal empowerment among minority students and their parents.

However, at another level, a very different process is operating. This opposing process is dedicated to maintaining the power structure within the society; in other words, preserving the current ways in which power is divided according to class, ethnicity, race and gender (as illustrated, for example, in job status). The existence of this opposing process can be inferred from the empirical data. To take a recent example related to women's rights, why does a nation that prides itself on its commitment to equality refuse to extend this equality to women, as illustrated by the failure to pass the Equal Rights Amendment?

In the same way, a powerful process operates to limit the extension of genuine equality of opportunity to class, racial and ethnic minorities. Maintenance of the societal power structure requires that the impact of attempts to empower minority students and communities be neutralized. This process must be inferred to explain why there is minimal public funding for those programs that have demonstrated their effectiveness in educating minority students, namely, programs that promote additive bilingualism through empowerment pedagogy.

Disempowerment of teachers constitutes part of the process whereby minority students are disempowered, since disempowered teachers are scarcely in a position to undertake empowerment pedagogy. As discussed previously, the current educational reform movement has contributed significantly to the disempowerment of teachers while sanctions against teachers who encourage students to develop their linguistic talents have the same effect. One consequence of this process is the victimization of the many thousands of teachers dedicated to genuinely educating minority students. The efforts of these teachers in the classroom and community are frustrated by forces beyond their control.

Naturally, the operation of this disempowerment process must be denied if it is to achieve its goals. The means through which this denial is achieved are almost identical to the disinformation and mystification techniques used by the Reagan administration to legitimate its attempt to overthrow the Nicaraguan government. The similarities between the domestic and international disempowerment process are considered below.

The Suppression of Empowerment among Domestic Minorities

Goals. The focus of the analysis in this section is on the rhetoric used to justify continued control and exploitation as being in the best interests of those groups against whom this control and exploitation is directed. In the case of the bilingual education debate, the covert goal of the dominant group is to effect a return to submersion programs to lessen the possibility that an even larger number of Hispanics will "get inside the door," to use Rodriguez' phrase; in other words, the goal is to continue the historical pattern of economic exploitation or in Ogbu's (1978) terms, to maintain the "job ceiling" for dominated minorities.

As mentioned in Chapter 2, it is striking that the minority groups in North America, Europe, and Asia that tend to experience disproportionate school failure are predominantly those that have experienced a pattern of subjugation over generations. As pointed out by Moore (1984),

"Education has been a commodity of freedom that European colonizers tended to deny to colonized people not because they could not consume education, but because educated colonized peoples would more quickly consume the colonial system. It was a crime in the United States to teach Black slaves to read, not because people of African descent were incapable of reading, but because reading would, as Frederick Douglass's master put it, 'unfit them to be slaves'.

When schooling has been provided in colonial settings, such as among native peoples in North America, it has often been another device to assault the fabric of indigenous societies, attacking and trying to supplant the language, values, belief systems and cultures that hold people together, while obliterating their history and glorifying that of white men" (p. 42).[3]

Empowerment pedagogy will continue to be resisted, despite the veneer of liberal reforms within the education system, because empowered peoples are more difficult to exploit. They are more likely to strike for better wages and working conditions, more likely to resist being sprayed with pesticides and fertilizers while picking fruit or vegetables and more likely to demand

---

[3]I am reminded here of Mahatma Gandhi's response when a reporter asked him what he thought about western civilization. Gandhi replied that he thought it would be an excellent idea.

a decent schooling for their children.[4] Consider, for example, this account of the Pajaro Valley family literacy project, described in Chapter 6:

> "Another parent said she noticed her children are now starting to request that she bring more books home to read, and they are now requesting them in Spanish instead of English. The result, she said, is they are learning about their culture and language, and also realizing that there are as many good ideas in Spanish as there are in English.
>
> Another parent said the reading and writing program has helped her to be more resolute in dealing with teachers and demanding that they teach her child Spanish, her native language.
>
> The biggest benefit, however, may be that the children and their parents are being drawn closer by the constant expression and discussion of ideas and books they are working on together.
>
> 'Tell your children every day how much you love them, how much you value them and how much you appreciate them,' Ada said in closing" (Estrada, Santa Cruz Sentinel, Friday Oct. 31, 1986).

It is clear that these parents are becoming empowered in the sense of gaining the internal resources, confidence and motivation to begin to exert some control over the forces that affect their lives. The notion of empowerment is similar to what Johan Galtung (1980), the Norwegian peace researcher and Director of the Centre of International Studies at Princeton University, calls *autonomy*, which is defined as follows:

> "Autonomy is here seen as power-over-oneself so as to be able to withstand what others might have of power-over-others. I use the distinction between ideological, remunerative and punitive power, depending on whether the influence is based on internal, positive external, or negative external sanctions. Autonomy then is the degree of 'inoculation' against these forms of power. These forms of power, exerted by means of ideas, carrots and sticks, can work only if the power receiver really receives the pressure, which presupposes a certain degree of submissiveness,

---

[4] An excellent ESL program for adults designed to raise students' consciousness of social factors that affect their lives is *ESL for Action: Problem-Posing at Work* by Elsa Roberts Auerbach and Nina Wallerstein, Addison-Wesley, 1987.

dependency and fear, respectively. Their antidotes are self-respect, self-sufficiency, and fearlessness. ... 'self-respect' can be defined as 'confidence in one's own ideas and ability to set one's own goals,' 'self-sufficiency' as the 'possibility of pursuing them with one's own means,' and 'fearlessness,' as 'the possibility of persisting despite threats of destruction. ...

The opposite [of autonomy] is penetration, meaning that the outside has penetrated into one's self to the extent of creating submissiveness to ideas, dependency on 'goods' from the outside, and fear of the outside in terms of 'bads.'" (1980, p. 58-59).

The resistence of many women to the Equal Rights Amendment during the 1980's is a good example of how the process of internalizing submissiveness and dependency works. Why else would so many women collaborate in maintaining a power structure that denies them equal rights? Similarly, as illustrated in Chapter 2, societal institutions such as schools have reinforced the unequal division of power by convincing minority students of their own inferiority, a process that results in submissiveness, dependency and fear, i.e. a lack of power-over-oneself or what Galtung terms "autonomy."

In Galtung's terms, empowerment pedagogy will be resisted by the dominant group because it results in self-respect, self-sufficiency and fearlessness; expressed in more conventional terms, it promotes minority students' self-esteem, ability for independent learning rather than learned helplessness, and confidence in their own academic and personal talents. By doing this, it reduces or eliminates the power of the dominant group to penetrate or control the formerly dominated minority group.

Process. Much of the debate in the United States (and in other western countries - see Skutnabb-Kangas, 1984) about the education of minority children is directed to obscuring contradictions between the rhetoric of equality and the reality of domination. Thus, programs aimed at preserving the learned helplessness of minority children (e.g. submersion under the guise of structured immersion) must be rationalized as being in the best interests of minority children; in addition, programs that empower children must either be eliminated through denial of funding or their impact controlled through media manipulation. In other words, the "threat of a good example" (Chomsky, 1987a) must be neutralized (see Table 8-1). This process involves at least three components:

• limiting the framework of discourse;

- denying/distorting empirically documented counter-examples;

- ignoring logical inconsistencies in the positions being advocated.

Limiting the Framework of Discourse. This process was noted in Chapter 7 with reference to the Baker and de Kanter report and the Gersten and Woodward articles, both of which strongly advocated structured immersion over transitional bilingual education. Despite the almost universal endorsement by researchers of enrichment bilingual programs (Fishman, 1976) designed to develop full bilingualism among both minority and majority students, enrichment programs have been effectively excluded from the policy debate. Thus the "threat of a good example," i.e. of enrichment programs empowering minority students, is contained, partly as a result of enrichment programs having little possibility of being funded and partly because any successful enrichment program will be classified as either transitional bilingual education or structured immersion (or both, as in the case of Legaretta [1979] in the Baker/de Kanter report). Thus its positive results can be aggregated out of existence in the midst of mediocre results from emasculated transitional programs.

The process of eliminating the threat of a good example by limiting the framework of discourse is well illustrated in the funding policies of the U.S. Department of Education in the final phase of the Reagan Administration (see *Education Week*, November 23, 1988). Grant recipients have been effectively prohibited from using grant monies to attend conferences of the National Association for Bilingual Education (NABE) since 1986 in an obvious move to put financial pressure on the main advocacy group for bilingual children.[5] One of the reasons for attempting to squeeze NABE financially is that NABE has been advocating for "developmental" programs (i.e. two-way enrichment bilingual programs) which are regarded as a threat by Education Department officials because they succeed so well in promoting English skills in addition to additive bilingualism for both minority and English-background students (see Genesee, 1987a, 1987b). I quote here at length from the *Education Week* report in order to illustrate how the rhetoric of equality is used to obscure the reality of disempowerment:

"Advocates and legislators also say they are disappointed in

---

[5]Alicia C. Coro, director of the office of bilingual education and minority-language affairs (OBEMLA) is reported to have said that "as long as I am head of OBEMLA, not a dime of federal money will go to support NABE" (Education Week, Nov. 23, 1988, p. 15).

the department's decision not to invite applications this year for developmental programs, which can include English-speaking students and seek to develop bilingualism as well as to teach English. ... The refusal to consider funding developmental efforts, say critics, is at odds with the Administration's position in favor of local flexibility. But only two developmental programs have ever received grants, both in 1985. ... Legislative backers of the developmental approach argue that it can help fill the nation's need for workers proficient in foreign languages, as well as helping L.E.P. [limited English proficient] children. 'An English-only mentality threatens to undercut the ability of our businessmen, soldiers, and diplomats to work effectively in today's world,' Represeatative Matthew G. Martinez, Democrat of California, said last week. Ms. Coro said that developmental bilingual education is 'a fantastic idea' but that the department wants to concentrate the limited amount of available funds in programs that serve only L.E.P. children. 'This is a great concept and I support that concept, but the demand [for grants] is so great that the bulk of the money must go for aiding the L.E.P. children,' she said (*Education Week*, 1988, Nov. 23, p. 14).

Denying/Distorting Empirically Documented Counter-Examples. There are several ways in which this has been done in the bilingual education debate. The Baker/de Kanter report set up highly questionable criteria of what they would accept with respect to methodological controls and managed to dismiss many apparently positive results from bilingual programs as a result. More significant, however, is the refusal to examine the research data with respect to its consistency with the theoretical assumptions underlying policy. This refusal permits opponents of bilingual education to ignore the fact that *virtually all* the data they analyze is inconsistent with the assumptions underlying structured immersion but consistent with those underlying enrichment (empowerment) bilingual programs. This disinformation appears to be effectively internalized by those spreading it such that they have become blind to what the data are saying. This is illustrated by Gersten and Woodward (1985a) when they address what they term "the paradox of transitional bilingual education":

"Lambert's argument touches what seems to be a logical paradox in the model: if students do not begin to read in English until the 2nd or 3rd grade, how will they ever catch up with their English-speaking peers?" (1980, p. 76).

This rhetorical question illustrates a split-brain logic that would be laughable if its impact were not so tragic for minority children. Gersten and Woodward are clearly familiar with Lambert's (and many others') documentation of the fact that students in Canadian French immersion programs who are not introduced to English language arts until grades 2 or 3 *invariably* catch up rapidly in English. In fact, they use these data to argue for "structured immersion" for minorities in the United States. They are also aware that virtually *all* the data reviewed by Baker and de Kanter (1981) showed children in bilingual programs performing at least as well in English as equivalent children in all-English programs, despite considerably less English exposure. Thus, lack of English instruction in the early grades is clearly not an impediment to English achievement, as documented in Chapter 4 of this volume. Yet the rhetorical question suggests that these data do not exist and, in fact, that the research data show the opposite of this. It appears to be impossible for Gersten and Woodward to see the reality of what the research is saying through the haze imposed by their sociopolitical assumptions and the direct instruction model. The split-brain logic involves justifying their argument on the basis of empirical data (i.e. French immersion programs, Baker and de Kanter's review) while ignoring the fact that all of this empirical data contradicts the assumptions underlying their position.

Ignoring Logical Inconsistencies. Three such inconsistencies can be noted. First, during the past decade a variety of influential groups and agencies within the United States have documented the "crisis" facing the United States as a result of its appalling incompetence in foreign languages. Both international trade and national security are jeopardized by the fact that, in the words of former Secretary of Education, Terrell Bell, American schools are producing "a bunch of monolinguistic bumpkins." Even avowed opponents of bilingual education such as Secretary of Education Bennett and members of the U.S. English organization proclaim themselves to be strongly in favor of improved foreign language programs.

The logic here is that we first ensure that schools eradicate students' native "foreign" language skills and then spend significant amounts of money trying to teach these same "foreign" language skills to these same students using traditional non-bilingual methods that have been demonstrated to be ineffective except for a small elite of students. This squandering of the nation's human resources hardly constitutes "excellence" in education. A nation that bases its education system on this type of logic is truly "at risk."

A second logical contradiction concerns the use made of the French immersion results to argue for "structured immersion". The logic here is to argue for a monolingual English-only program, taught largely by monolingual teachers, and aimed at producing monolingualism, on the basis of the success of a program involving full bilingual instruction, taught by bilingual teachers, whose explicit goal is to produce additive bilingualism and biliteracy.

A third logical contradiction involves the push to exit children from transitional programs as quickly as possible. The logic here is that children have been put into bilingual programs on the grounds that they will make better English academic progress in a bilingual rather than a monolingual program. In other words, less English instruction will lead to more English achievement. As noted earlier, the empirical data are consistent with this assumption. Yet the rationale behind exiting students as quickly as possible is that they will fall behind in English unless they are in a program with maximum exposure to English. In other words, the two rationales are logically inconsistent with each other.

The extent of the logical contradiction here can be seen in the fact that minority students in the early grades of transitional programs are expected to make so much progress in the cognitive/academic skills underlying English literacy that after a short period they should be able to compete on an equal footing with their monolingual English-speaking peers who have had all their instruction through English. In other words, the quicker the exit from transitional programs, the more effective one must logically assume that the bilingual program has been in developing English proficiency. If these programs are so effective in promoting English, then what is the educational logic in exiting the child at all?

These logical contradictions and the denial/distortion of evidence promoting empowerment programs illustrate the process whereby the veneer of equity is maintained on the structure that disables minority children. In Galtung's terms, this structure provides the dominant group with "power-over-others" while denying dominated groups (whether children in classrooms or migrant workers in fields) the opportunity to develop "power-over-self."

The process is the same as that which has been pursued, with far more hideous results, by many powerful nations in their exploitation of less powerful nations.[6]

Eliminating the Threat of a Good Example in the International Arena

The same processes of (a) limiting the framework of discourse, (b) denying/distorting empirically documented counter-examples, and (c) ignoring logical inconsistencies are evident in the ways in which powerful countries have historically legitimized their domination of weaker countries (e.g. Britain over Ireland for centuries). The current Central American situation illustrates well the operation of these processes.

Some Empirical Data. Most Americans are by now vaguely aware of the mass disappearances of suspected dissidents and the hideous torture that is commonplace in the majority of Latin American countries. For example, the Amnesty International report for 1975-76 noted that more than 80% of the urgent appeals for victims of human torture have been coming from Latin America and the situation has not improved markedly during the past decade. Americans are also aware, in a vague way, of the CIA's involvement in Latin America during the past 35 or so years, ostensibly in order to promote democracy and prevent the spread of communism. The American aid to the Contra rebels in Nicaragua is seen as part of this tradition of supporting the spread of democracy and resisting communist expansion, a threat that is not only against but anathema to "American concepts." The consequences of failing to support the "democratic resistence" in Nicaragua were vividly painted by Col. North in his testimony before the Iran-Contra committee on July 13, 1987:

> "You will see democracy perish in Central America, a flood of refugees trying to cross our borders and potentially the construction of a Berlin-type wall to keep people out" (Toronto Star, July 14, 1987, A15).

---

[6]The primary example taken here is of the Reagan administration's war against Nicaragua, mainly because this is an ongoing issue familiar to most minority communities and bilingual educators. However, any number of other historical or current examples involving the Soviet Union, Britain, France, and most other powerful countries, could have been chosen. For example, historically, the American and Irish revolutionary struggles against British domination and exploitation are no different in principle than the struggles of Afgan guerillas against Soviet exploitation or of the Sandinista guerillas against the brutally oppressive Somoza regime. In all cases, the struggle is an attempt to assert autonomy or "power-over-oneself." See Phillipson and Skutnabb-Kangas, 1986, for an insightful analysis of the historical and current manipulation of language policies by colonial powers as a means of reinforcing domination and exploitation of colonized groups.

Polls indicated that this message was believed by a large proportion of Americans with more than 90% of those polled supporting North's actions and many wanting him to run for President.

What was striking to many Europeans and Canadians about North's testimony was the total acceptance by the committee (as indicated by the lack of questions) of the demonstrably false presuppositions underlying North's actions and testimony.

In the first place, despite the rhetoric of "democratization" and freedom, CIA-inspired foreign policy does not appear to have been particularly concerned about democracy. For example, over a 40 year period, the United States supported the dictatorship of General Somoza in Nicaragua whose brutality gave rise to the Sandinista resistance. Thus, in an important sense, the Sandinista revolution is the offspring of U.S. foreign policy.

Another point that, not surprisingly, was not raised at the Iran-Contra hearings is the fact that the CIA has systematically inspired military coups against democratically-elected governments in Latin America and elsewhere that have attempted to initiate even mild social changes (e.g. land reform) or were not felt to be sympathetic to the profit needs of multinational companies. For example, the democratically-elected government of Jacobo Arbenz in Guatemala was ousted by a CIA-inspired coup in 1954. Since that time the military dictatorship has been responsible for at least 100,000 people murdered, 38,000 disappearances and 200,000 refugees (Wright, 1987). Democratic elections were held in 1985 but the elected president Vinicio Cerezo, "exists only on the generals sufferance, a fact he makes no attempt to deny" (Wright, 1987, p. 50). Democratically-elected governments in Brazil (1964) and Chile (1973) were also overthrown as a result of CIA-supported coups (see Black, 1977) and thousands of men, women and children were tortured and/or disappeared as a result of this "democratization" process.

The rhetoric of "democratization" in the war against Nicaragua grows even hollower in view of the fact that many of the Contra "freedom fighters" are former Somoza troops responsible for the human rights abuses in Nicaragua that gave rise to the revolution in the first place.[7]

A further point is that Nicaragua is one of the few countries in Latin America that can make any credible claim to have a democratically elected government. In the general elections of 1984, the Sandinista party won 61 of the 96 seats in the Assembly, the others being shared between 6 other parties, four to the right of the Sandinistas and two to the left (see Rushdie, 1987). The vast majority of international observers of these elections, including the professional association of U.S. Latin America scholars (LASA), described them as remarkably open and honest. The failure of any members of the Iran-Contra committee to question Col. North on his interpretation of the term "democracy" (and his patently false assumption that it exists elsewhere in Central America but not in Nicaragua) supports Chomsky's (1987a) claim that the LASA detailed report and those of other international observers "were virtually suppressed in the United States, where the 1984 elections did not take place, according to the government-media consensus" (p. 85).

The Iran-Contra committee was also largely silent on the morality and legality of U.S. involvement in Nicaragua. For example, no mention was made of the International Court at the Hague's ruling that the U.S. was liable to pay reparation for the estimated $2 billion worth of economic damage inflicted against Nicaragua by the U.S.-backed war. No mention was made in the hearings of the appropriateness of the "democratization" process in view of the social progress made in Nicaragua in comparison to that of neigboring countries. Chomsky summarizes the conclusions of two Oxfam reports and that of the World Bank as follows:

"The charitable development agency Oxfam America ... observed in 1985 that among the countries of the region where Oxfam works (Guatemala, El Salvador, Honduras and Nicaragua) 'only in Nicaragua has a substantial effort been

---

[7]Unsavory aspects of the "democratic resistence" tend to be quickly glossed over in the media. One hears little of accounts such as the following description by Salman Rushdie of a village called Blue Lagoon on the east coast of Nicaragua: "Round the corner from Miss Pancha's was the house of a young couple who were selling up and moving to Bluefields (a larger town on the east coast) because the Contras had killed the man's father. In almost every house you could hear a tale of death. Even one of the local Moravian priests had been killed. In a nearby village, the Contra had recently kidnapped more than two dozen children, many of them girls aged between ten and fourteen, 'for the use of the Contra fighters' Mary told me. One girl escaped and got home. The villagers had heard that five other children had escaped, but had been lost in the jungle. That was five weeks ago and they had to be presumed dead" (1987 p. 138-139). Salman Rushdie based his description of the Nicaraguan situation both on analysis of documentary evidence and three weeks spent travelling through Nicaragua in July 1986. He is the recipient of several prestigious literary awards and a Fellow of the Royal Society of Literature in Britain.

made to address inequities in land ownership and to extend health, educational, and agricultural services to poor peasant families' though the contra war - fulfilling its objectives - 'has slowed the pace of social reform and compounded hunger in the northern countryside'. ... the parent organization of Oxfam in London went still further, declaring Nicaragua to be "exceptional" among 76 countries where Oxfam has worked in the government's commitment 'to improving the condition of the people and encouraging their active participation in the development process' thus posing what Oxfam accurately terms 'the threat of a good example'. The World Bank described the dedication of the government to improving the lives of the poor as 'remarkable' (June 1983), and identified its projects in Nicaragua as among the best it had supported, noting the absence of corruption and the concern for the poor" (1987a, p. 84).

Chomsky identifies a major reason why none of these facts are part of the American consciousness about Nicaragua, namely, the role of the press and other media in screening the American public from such details. He notes, for example, that in the first three months of 1986, the New York Times and Washington Post ran 85 pieces by columnists and invited contributors, virtually all of which were highly critical of the Sandinistas. The two most striking features of the Sandinista regime, namely the constructive social programs and the absence of large-scale torture and slaughter (unlike most other Latin American countries) were almost entirely ignored in the articles. A similar finding emerged in an analysis Chomsky conducted on 80 New York Times editorials between 1980 and 1986.

What has this got to do with the struggle for minority student empowerment within the United States? With respect to goals and methods, the process of systematic disempowerment of dominated groups, whether internal or external to the United States, has been essentially the same. In both cases, there has been an economic dimension to the exploitation and in both cases, a strong sense of paranoia has been generated about presumed threats to the American way of life. To many observers, the idea that a country as tiny and as economically-weak as Nicaragua could constitute a threat to the most powerful nation in the world appears as ludicrous as the likelihood of a Hispanic separatist movement. However, the paranoia engendered by both these "threats" is strong and this paranoia results in policies and practices of questionable morality to counteract the threat. In order to counteract both the domestic and international "threats", violations of human rights (e.g. destabilizing the economies of weaker nations, destabilizing the personal and academic development of minority students) are veiled in the rhetoric of equality and justice, as they always have been by dominant groups everywhere. The rhetoric is no different in essence than the rhetoric of "the white man's burden" used to justify colonization and exploitation of developing nations under the guise of promoting democracy, civilizing the natives, saving heathen souls, etc (see Table 8-1).

In both situations, the three strategies identified above with respect to the bilingual education debate are very much in evidence; namely, (a) limiting the framework of discourse, (b) denying/distorting empirical realities, and (c) ignoring logical contradictions. Just as in the bilingual education debate where the options have been narrowed to transitional bilingual education versus structured immersion, the options facing the American people in Nicaragua (and elsewhere around the world) are narrowed to "communist aggression" versus "freedom". In both situations it is "us" against "them" and "they" are threatening to encroach on "our" power (usually expressed in terms of "our way of life"). The empirical data in both situations are cynically misrepresented and distorted by the media and policy-makers, and logical inconsistencies are glossed over as either non-existent or irrelevant (which in a sense they are given the generally non-critical response of the public to such "details").[8]

The analogies in the two situations can be described in terms of Galtung's distinction between power-over-others and power-over-self (i.e. autonomy). As a result of the fact that the Nicaraguans managed to achieve (at least partially) a position of power-over-themselves, they negated the previous U.S. dominance and threatened to further reduce U.S. power-over-others by the "threat of a good example," i.e. a left-wing democratic government effectively promoting literacy and social justice. This has generated a renewed attempt by the U.S. to penetrate the previously controlled country and restore its power-over-others by means of

---

[8]It is worth noting that some members of the Iran-Contra committee did pick up the inconsistency between the "totalitarian" methods used by Col. North and the goal of "democracy" which these methods were intended to achieve but they were referring more to the internal problems of breaking the law, lying to Congress, altering national security documents, etc, than to the assault on a democratic government being conducted in order to "democratize" that country. A further tragic irony of this process is that historical precedent in Guatemala, Iran, Brazil, and Chile would suggest that the success of the Contra counter-revolution would in all likelihood restore Nicaragua to the horrors of the Somoza regime which butchered the poor of Nicaragua for 40 years. Again, there is an analogy both in goal and process with the attempt to restore submersion programs for minority children under the label of structured immersion.

Table 8-1

**Neutralizing the Threat of a Good Example in
Preserving Global and Domestic Power Structures**

A. GOAL

Ensure that the economic and political interests of the dominant group are not threatened by deviant initiatives that might empower emergent nations or minority groups.

B. METHOD

Exert economic and political pressure to ensure that implementation of the deviant initiative is destabilized and outcomes are negative. If positive outcomes emerge despite this pressure, then either ignore, deny or distort them.

C. OUTCOMES

The failure of the deviant initiative under these conditions will demonstrate that attempts at dominated group empowerment are ill-conceived and ill-advised. Dominant group control can be re-established under the guise of equality and justice.

punitive power (military force).[9]

For generally similar reasons of social control and reproduction, power-over-self or empowerment has not been identified as a goal of any of the special programs designed to help minorities (e.g. compensatory education, bilingual education) nor of the broader educational reform movement. For purposes of societal reproduction, indoctrination through transmission approaches to pedagogy is a more desirable educational outcome than empowerment and critical thinking. As Freire has shown, communities that become conscious of their social disenfrancisement or of a discriminatory social situation are likely to directly challenge the institutional power structure and become further empowered as a result of this challenge.[10]

This process is illustrated by the school strike organized by Finnish parents and their children at Bredby school in Rinkeby, Sweden. In response to a plan by the headmistress to reduce the amount of Finnish instruction and the failure of protest through "approved" channels, the Finnish community withdrew their children from the school. Eventually (after eight weeks) most of their demands were met. According to Skutnabb-Kangas (1985, 1988), the strike had the effect of generating a new sense of efficacy among the community and making them aware of the role of dominant-group controlled education in reproducing the powerless status of minority groups. Skutnabb-Kangas describes the process through which the parents progressed from dependency to self-sufficiency, from submissiveness to self-respect, and from fear to fearlessness; in short, they developed to a stage where they refused to be power-receivers.

Another recent example comes from Canada and involves the negotiations between the Lubicon Indians and both federal and provincial (Alberta) governments regarding a land settlement. While both levels of government agreed that the 477-member band was entitled to a reserve, negotiations had repeatedly foundered (for almost 50 years!) over the question of its size. Meanwhile oil companies were making large profits (and contributing substantial provincial royalties) on lands claimed by the Lubicon band. Finally, frustrated with the constant stalling by the

---

[9]It is arguable that the long-term use of remunerative power (i.e. "goods") would have been considerably more effective in restoring economic dependency on the U.S. than the punitive power used in Nicaragua.

[10]Freire's expulsion from Brazil after the 1964 CIA-inspired coup was a result of the accurate perception of the totalitarian government that his "liberation pedagogy" constituted a potentially serious threat to their power-over-others.

provincial government, the Lubicon on October 15, 1988, declared themselves a sovereign nation (which legally they may be since they had never signed a treaty surrendering their lands or sovereignty) and barricaded the access highway to their lands. Oil companies were required to pay for access to the 300 or so wells in the area. Only at this point did things begin to happen. Supporters and the media arrived from several European countries and also from different parts of Canada. Among those lending legitimacy to the band's declaration of autonomy (in Galtung's sense) were representatives of the United, Anglican, Presbyterian, Evangelical Lutheran, Mennonite, Quaker, and Roman Catholic churches. Under these circumstances, physical confrontation between the tiny band and the police would have been disastrous public relations for the governments both domestically (because of an upcoming federal election) and internationally.[11] Within a week of establishing the blockade, all the band's demands were met. What 48 years of "due process" could not resolve was accomplished by a well-timed assertion of power-over-self (see, for example, *The Globe and Mail*, October 20, 1988).

Conclusion

In this final chapter, I have tried to put the research issues in the area of bilingual education into the context of their relevance for genuine change in the education of minority children. By genuine change, I mean change in the disabling structure rather than change in the appearance of that structure. The structure of institutionalized racism that assaults minority students' cultural identity in schools and prevents empowerment is essentially the same structure in goals and functions as the structure that has attempted to maintain a "favorable climate" in third world countries for continued profitability for multinational companies. Totalitarian regimes that have continued to provide a favorable climate for multinational investment have not been challenged (e.g. Pinochet's Chile) whereas democratically-elected governments that are considered "leftist" are either overthrown (e.g. Allende's Chile) or destabilized (e.g. Nicaragua).

The domestic process whereby minorities are disempowered is clearly no longer overt in the same way as the international process. However, the covert racism and psychological violence to which dominated minority

---

[11]Indian leaders from elsewhere in Canada had already embarrassed the federal government by travelling to South Africa to publicize the deplorable plight of many Indian groups across Canada. Further international attention to the health and educational problems of Canada's Indians would have greatly reduced the credibility of Canada's image as a strong promoter of human rights internationally.

students are still subjected represents the same essential process to which previous generations of students were subjected in more physically violent form. The rhetoric and disinformation remains the same, albeit more sophisticated, as required by the relatively more easy access to information in the 1980's.

Resistence to this process requires that communities become aware of the nature of the forces that continue to subjugate them and the means through which this subjugation is achieved; for example, through ideological, remunerative and punitive exercise of power-over-others. Educators and policy-makers must also become conscious of these same forces if they are to develop partnerships with community groups to more effectively challenge the disabling structure.

From this perspective, those committed to empowerment bilingual education are far more patriotic (in a genuine sense of the term) than those opposed in that they are taking seriously and trying to implement the principles of equality, justice, and freedom (i.e. power-over-self) upon which the American state was founded. Among those who oppose empowerment bilingual education, concerns about equality and justice are often less prominent than concerns about "threats posed to whites by rapid population growth among Hispanics" (in the terms used by former U.S. English Chairman John Tanton). By the same token, educators who promote children's bilingual skills are contributing to the creation of a linguistically-competent nation, and to its security and economic interests, far more than those who attempt to eradicate these language skills. Eradicating children's linguistic talents contributes only to the creation of a nation of "monolinguistic bumpkins" (in the words of former Education Secretary Terrell Bell) that is internationally isolated and subject to mutual misunderstanding with other nations.

In short, in order to reverse the pattern of minority group school failure and contribute to a stronger nation, educators and policy-makers are faced with both a personal and political challenge. Personally, they must redefine their roles within the classroom, the community and the broader society so that these role definitions result in interactions that empower rather than disable students. Politically, they must attempt to persuade colleagues and decision-makers - such as school boards and the public that elects them - of the importance of redefining institutional goals so that the schools transform society by empowering minority students rather than reflect society by disabling them.

REFERENCES

Ada, A.F. 1986, Creative education for bilingual teachers. *Harvard Educational Review*, *56*, 386-394.

Ada, A.F. 1988a, Creative reading: A relevant methodology for language minority children. In L.M. Malave (Ed.) *NABE '87. Theory, research and application: Selected Papers.* Buffalo: State University of New York.

Ada, A.F. 1988b, The Pajaro Valley experience: Working with Spanish-speaking parents to develop children's reading and writing skills in the home through the use of children's literature. In T. Skutnabb-Kangas and J. Cummins (Ed.), *Minority education: From shame to struggle.* Clevedon, England: Multilingual Matters.

Ada, A.F. & de Olave, M. de P. 1986, *Hagamos caminos*. Reading, MA: Addison Wesley.

American Psychological Association, 1982, Review of Department of Education report entitled "Effectiveness of bilingual education: A review of the literature". Letter to Congressional Hispanic Caucus, April 22.

Association for Supervision and Curriculum Development (ASCD), 1987, *Building an indivisible nation: Bilingual education in context.* Alexandria, Virginia: ASCD.

Auerbach, E.R. & Wallerstein, N. 1987, *ESL for action: Problem posing at work.* Reading, Mass: Addison-Wesley.

Baker, K.A. & de Kanter, A.A. 1981, *Effectiveness of Bilingual Education: A Review of the Literature.* Washington, D.C.: Office of Planning and Budget, U.S. Department of Education.

Balesse, L. & Freinet, C. 1971, *La lectura en la escuela por medio de la imprenta.* Barcelona: Editorial Laia.

Barnes, D. 1976, *From Communication to Curriculum.* Harmondsworth: Penguin.

Becker, W.C. 1977, Teaching reading and languge to the disadvantaged: What we have learned from field research. *Harvard Educational Review*, *47*, 518-543.

Beers, C.S. & Beers, J.W. 1980, Early identification of learning disabilities: Facts and fallacies. *The Elementary School Journal*, *81*, 67-76.

Bereiter, C., Englemann, S., Osborn, J. & Reidford, P.A., 1966, An academically-oriented preschool for culturally deprived children. In F. Hechinger (Ed.) *Preschool education today.* New York: Doubleday.

Berger, T. 1977, *Northern frontier, northern homeland: The report of the Mackenzie Valley Pipeline Inquiry.* Vol. 1. Toronto: James Lorimer and Co.

Bethell, T. 1979, Against bilingual education. *Harper's*, February.

Bhatnagar, J. 1980, Linguistic behaviour and adjustment of immigrant children in french and English schools in Montreal. *International Review of applied Psychology, 29*, 141-149.

Biber, D. 1986, Spoken and written textual dimensions in English: Resolving the contradictory findings. *Language, 62*, 384-414.

Black, J.K. 1977, *United States penetration of Brazil.* University of Pennsylvania Press.

Brisk, M.E. 1985, Using the computer to develop literacy. *Equity and Choice, 1*, 25-32.

Brophy, J.E. & Good, T.L. 1974, *Teacher-student relationships: Cause and consequences.* New York: Holt, Rinehart and Winston.

Bullock Report. 1975, *A Language for life: Report of the Committee of inquiry appointed by the Secretary of State for Education and Science under the chairmanship of Sir Alan Bullock.* London: HMSO.

California State Department of Education, 1985, *Case studies in bilingual education: First Year Report.* Federal Grant #G008303723.

Campos, J. & Keatinge, R., 1988, The Carpinteria language minority student experience: From theory, to practice, to success. In T. Skutnabb-Kangas and J. Cummins (Ed.), *Minority education: From shame to struggle.* Clevedon, England: Multilingual Matters.

Carlisle, R.S. 1986, *The writing of Anglo and Hispanic fourth and sixth graders in regular, submersion, and bilingual programs.* Doctoral dissertation, University of Illinois at Urbana-Champaign. Dissertation Abstracts International, *47*, no. 9, 1987.

Carter, T.P. 1970, *Mexican-Americans at school: A history of educational neglect.* New York: College Entrance Examination Board.

Chomsky, C. 1981, Write now, read later. In C. Cazden (Ed.) *Language in early childhood education, 2nd ed.).* Washington, D.C.: National Association for the Education of Young Children.

Chomsky, N. 1987a, *On power and ideology: The Managua lectures.* Boston: South End Press.

Chomsky, N. 1987b, *The Chomsky reader.* Edited by James Peck. New York: Pantheon.

Chomsky, N. & Herman, E.S. 1979, *The Washington connection and third world fascism: The political economy of human rights, Volume 1.* Montreal: Black Rose Books.

Clarizio, H.F. 1982, Intellectual assessment of Hispanic children. *Psychology in the Schools, 19,* 61-71.

Cohen, D.K. 1970, Immigrants and the schools. *Review of Educational Research, 40,* 13-27.

Cohen, A.D. & Swain, M. 1976, Bilingual education: The immersion model in the North American context. *TESOL Quarterly, 10,* 45-53.

Coles, G.S. 1978, The learning disabilities test battery: Empirical and social issues. *Harvard Educational Review, 48,* 313-340.

Collier, V.P. 1987, Age and rate of acquisition of second language for academic purposes. *TESOL Quarterly, 21,* 617-641.

Collier, V.P. & Thomas, W.P. 1988, Acquisition of cognitive-academic second language proficiency: A six-year study. Paper presented at the American Educational Research Association, New Orleans, April.

Crawford, J. 1986, Immersion method is faring poorly in bilingual study. *Education Week, 5,* p. 1 and 10, April 23.

Crawford, J. 1988, *Bilingual education: History, politics, theory, and practice..* Trenton, NJ: Crane Publishing Co.

Cuban, L. 1984, School reform by remote control: SB 813 in California. *Phi Delta Kappan, 66,* 167-215.

Cummins, J. 1979, Linguistic interdependence and the educational development of bilingual children. *Review of Educational Research, 49,* 222-251.

Cummins, J. 1981a, The public image of bilingual education. Report submitted to the Ford Foundation, 1981.

Cummins, J. 1981b, The role of primary language development in promoting educational success for language minority students. In California State Department of Education (Ed.), *Schooling and language minority students: A theoretical framework*. Evaluation, Dissemination and Assessment Center, California State University, Los Angeles.

Cummins, J. 1981c, Age on arrival and immigrant second language learning in Canada: A reassessment. *Applied Linguistics, 2*, 132-149.

Cummins, J. 1983, *Heritage language education: A literature review*. Toronto: Ministry of Education, Ontario.

Cummins J. 1984, *Bilingualism and special education: Issues in assessment and pedagogy*. Clevedon, England: Multilingual Matters. Co-published in the United States by College-Hill Press, San Diego.

Cummins, J. 1986, Empowering minority students: A framework for intervention. *Harvard Education Review, 56*, 18-36. Cummins, J. et al. 1984,

Cummins, J. & Swain, M. 1986, *Bilingualism in education: Aspects of theory, research and practice*. London: Longman.

Cummins, J., Harley, B., Swain, M. & Allen, P.A, in press, Social and individual factors in the development of bilingual proficiency. In Harley, B., Allen, P.A., Cummins, J. & Swain, M. (EDs.), *The development of second language proficiency*. Cambridge: Cambridge University Press.

Curtis, J. 1988, Parents, schools and racism: A case study of bilingual education in a Northern California community. In T. Skutnabb-Kangas and J. Cummins (Ed.), *Minority education: From shame to struggle*. Clevedon, England: Multilingual Matters.

Daiute, C. 1985, *Writing and computers*. Reading, Mass.: Addison-Wesley.

Danoff, M.V., Coles, G.J., McLaughlin, D.H. & Reynolds, D.J. 1977,1978, *Evaluation of the impact of ESEA Title VII Spanish/English bilingual education program*. Palo Alto, CA: American Institutes for Reserch.

Darling-Hammond, L. 1985, Valuing teachers: The making of a profession. *Teachers College Record, 87,* 209-218.

DeAvila, E., Cohen, E.G., & Intili, J.A. Multicultural improvement of cognitive abilities. Final report to California State Department of Education, 1981.

Diaz, R.M. 1986, Bilingual cognitive development: Addressing three gaps in current research. *Child Development.*

Dolson, D. 1985, The effects of Spanish home language use on the scholastic performance of Hispanic pupils. *Journal of Multilingual and Multicultural Development, 6,* 135-156.

Dunn, L. 1987, *Bilingual Hispanic children on the U.S. mainland: A review of research on their cognitive, linguistic, and scholastic development.* Circle Pines, Minesota: American Guidance Service.

Edelsky, C. 1981, From "Jimosalcsco" to "7 Narangas se calleron y et arbol-est-triste en lagrymas": Writing development in a bilingual program. In B. Cronnell (Ed.) *the writing needs of linguistically different students.* Los Alamitos, CA: Southwest Educational Development Laboratory.

Elley, W.B. 1981, Why teach a centipede to walk? *Education* (New Zealand), *3,* 11-13.

Englemann, S. & Osborn, J. 1976, *DISTAR language: An instructional system.* 2nd ed. Chicago: Science Research Associates.

Enright, D.S. & McCloskey, M.L. 1988, *Integrating English: Developing English language and literacy in the multilingual classroom.* Reading, Mass: Addison-Wesley.

Epstein, N. 1977, *Language, ethnicity and the schools.* Washington, D.C.: Institute for Educational Leadership.

Estrada, H.M. 1986, 'Pajaro experience' teaches parents how to teach kids. *Santa Cruz Sentinel,* Friday October 31, p. A4.

Fishman, J. 1976, Bilingual education: What and why? In J.E. Alatis and K. Twaddell (Eds.) *English as a second language in bilingual education.* Washington, D.C.: TESOL.

Freire, P. 1973, *Education for critical consciousness.* New York: Seabury.

Freire, P. 1983, Banking education. In H. Giroux and D. Purpel

(Eds.) *The hidden curriculum and moral education: Deception or discovery?*. Berkeley, CA: McCutcheon Publishing Corporation.

Freire, P. *The politics of education: Culture, power and liberation.* South Hadley, Mass: Bergin & Garvey.

Galtung, J. 1980, *The true worlds: A transnational perspective.* New York: The Free Press.

Genesee, F. 1985, Second language learning through immersion: A review of U.S. programs. *Review of Educational Research, 55,* 541-561.

Genesee, F. 1987a, *Learning through two languages: Studies of immersion and bilingual education.* Cambridge, Mass: Newbury House.

Genesee, F. 1987b, Considering two-way bilingual education. *Equity and Choice, 3,* 3-7.

Gersten, R. 1985, Structured immersion for language minority students: Results of a longitudinal evaluation. *Educational Evaluation and Policy Analysis, 7,* 187-196.

Gersten, R. & Woodward, J. 1985a, A case for structured immersion. *Educational Leadership,* September, 75-79.

Gersten, R. & Woodward, J. 1985b, Response to Santiago. *Educational Leadership,* September, 83-84.

Geva, E. & Ryan, E.B. 1987, Linguistic knowledge and cognitive demands for academic skills in first and second language. Manuscript submitted for publication, OISE, 1987.

Gill, D. & Levidow, L. 1987, *Anti-racist science teaching.* London: Free Association Books.

Giroux, H.A. & McLaren, P. 1986, Teacher education and the politics of engagement: The case for democratic schooling. *Harvard Educational Review, 56,* 213-238.

Glazer, N. & Cummins, J. 1985, Viewpoints on bilingual education. *Equity and Choice, 2,* 47-52.

Goldman, S.R. 1985, *Utilization of knowledge acquired through the first language in comprehending a second language: Narrative composition by Spanish-English speakers.* Report submitted to the U.S. Department of Education.

Goodlad, J.I. 1984, *A place called school: Prospects for the future.*

New York: McGraw Hill.

Goodman, K.S. & Goodman, Y.M. 1977, Learning about psycholinguistic processes by analysing oral reading. *Harvard Educational Review*, 47, 317-333.

Graves, D. 1978, *Balance the basics: Let them write.* Report submitted to the Ford Foundation.

Graves, D. 1983, *Writing: Children and teachers at work.* Exeter, NH: Heinemann.

Gray, T. 1977, Challenge to USOE final evaluation of the impact of ESEA Title VII Spanish/English bilingual education programs. Arlington, VA: Center for Applied Linguistics.

Guerra, V. 1984, *Predictors of second language learners' error judgements in written English.* Doctoral dissertation, University of Houston.

Hakuta, K. 1986, *The Mirror of Language: The Debate on Bilingualism.* New York: Basic Books.

Hakuta, K. & Diaz, R.M. 1985, The relationship between degree of bilingualism and cognitive ability: A critical discussion and some new longitudinal data. In K.E. Nelson (Ed.), *Children's Language, vol. 5* Hillsdale, New Jersey: Erlbaum.

Heath, S.B. 1983, *Ways with words.* Cambridge: Cambridge University Press.

Heath, S.B. 1986, Sociocultural contexts of language development. In California State Department of Education (Ed.), *Beyond language: Social and cultural factors in schooling language minority students.* Los Angeles: Evaluation, Dissemination, and Assessment Center.

Jensen, A.R. 1980, *Bias in mental testing.* New York: The Free Press.

Jusenius, C. & Duarte, V.L. 1982, *Hispanics and jobs: Barriers to progress.* Washington, D.C.: National Commission for Employment Policy.

Kagan, S. 1986, Cooperative learning and sociocultural factors in schooling. In California State Department of Education, *Beyond language: Social and cultural factors in schooling language minority students.* Los Angeles: Evaluation, Dissemination, and Assessement Center, California State University.

Katsaiti, L.T.   1983, *Interlingual transfer of a cognitive skill in bilinguals*. M.A. Thesis, Ontario institute for Studies in Education.

Kemp, J. 1984, *Native Language Knowledge as a Predictor of Success in Learning a foreign Language with Special reference to a Disadvantaged Population*.   Thesis submitted for the M.a. Degree, Tel-Aviv University.

Krashen, S.D.   1981, Bilingual education and second language acquisition theory.   In California State Department of Education, *Schooling and language minority students: A theoretical framework*.   Los Angeles: Evaluation, Dissemination and Assessment Center.

Krashen, S. 1982, *Principles and practice in second language acquisition*. New York: Pergamon Press.

Krashen, S. & Biber, D. 1988, *On course: Bilingual education's success in California*. Sacramento: California Association for Bilingual Education.

Labov, W. 1970, *The study of nonstandard English*.   Champaign, Illinois: National Council of Teachers of English.

Lambert, W.E. 1975, Culture and language as factors in learning and education.   In A. Wolfgang (Ed.), *Education of immigrant students*. Toronto: O.I.S.E.

Lambert, W.E. & Tucker, G.R. 1972, *Bilingual education of children: The St. Lambert Experiment.* Rowley, Mass.: Newbury House.

Legaretta, D. 1979, The effects of program models on language acquisition by Spanish speaking children. *TESOL Quarterly, 13*, 521-534.

Lindfors, J.W. 1980, *Children's language and learning.* Englewood Cliffs, New Jersey: Prentice Hall.

Long, M.H. 1983, Native speaker/non-native speaker conversation in the second language classroom.   In M.A. Clarke & J. Handscombe (eds.), *On TESOL '82: Pacific perspectives on language learning and teaching*. Washington D.C.: TESOL.

Lucas, I. 1981, Bilingual education and the melting pot: Getting burned. The Illinois Issues Humanities Essays: 5. Illinois Humanities Council, Champaign, Illinois.

McLaughlin, B. 1984, Early bilingualism: Methodological and

theoretical issues. In M. Paradis and Y. Lebrun (Eds.) *Early bilingualism and child development*. Lisse: Swets & Zeitlinger B.V.

McLaughlin, B. 1986, Multilingual education: Theory east and west. In B. Spolsky (Ed.) *Language and education in multilingual settings*. Clevedon, England: Multilingual Matters.

McLeod, A. 1986, Critical literacy: Taking control of our own lives. *Language Arts, 63*, 37-50.

Mehan, H., Miller-Souviney, B., & Riel, M.M. 1984, Knowledge of text editing and the development of literacy skills. *Language Arts, 65*, 154 -159.

Mehan, H., Hertweck, A., & Meihls, J.L. 1986, *Handicapping the handicapped: Decision making in students' educational careers*. Palo Alto: Stanford University Press.

Mehan, H. et al. 1986, *The write help: Resources and activities for word processing*. Glenview, Illinois: Scott Foresman and Company.

Mercer, J. 1973, *Labelling the mentally retarded*. Los Angeles: University of California.

Moore, R.B. 1984, School systems perpetuate racism and don't know it - can we deal with it? In Canadian Education Association (Ed.) *Multiculturalism, racism and the school system*. Toronto: Canadian Education Association.

National Assessment of Educational Progress, 1983, *Students from homes in which English is not the dominant language: who are they and how well do they read?* No. 11-R-50. Denver: Education Commission of the States.

New Zealand Department of Education, 1988, *New Voices: Second language learning and teaching. A handbook for primary teachers*. Wellington: Department of Education.

Ogbu, J.U. 1978, *Minority education and caste*. New York: Academic Press.

Ogbu, J.U. and Matute-Bianchi, M.E. 1986, Understanding sociocultural factors: Knowledge, identity and school adjustment. In California State Department of Education (Ed.), *Sociocultural factors and minority student achievement*. Los Angeles: Evaluation, Dissemination, and Assessement Center, California State University.

O'Malley, J.M. 1978, Review of the evaluation of the impact of ESEA Title VII Spanish/English bilingual education program. *Bilingual Resources*, *1*, 6-10.

Ortiz, A.A. & Yates, J.R. 1983, Incidence of exceptionality among Hispanics: Implications for manpower planning. *NABE Journal*, 7, 41-54.

Ovando, C.J. & Collier, V.P. 1985, *Bilingual and ESL classrooms: Teaching in multicultural contexts*. New York: McGraw-Hill Book Company.

Phillipson, R. & Skutnabb-Kangas, T. 1986, *Linguicism rules in education*. Doctoral dissertation submitted to Roskilde University, Denmark.

Platero, D. 1975, Bilingual education in the Navajo Nation. In R.C. Troike and N. Modiano (Eds.) *Proceedings of the First Inter-American Conference on Bilingual Education*. Arlington Va.: Center for Applied Linguistics.

Ramirez, C.M. 1985, *Bilingual education and language interdependence: Cummins and beyond*. Doctoral dissertation, Yeshiva University.

Ravitch, D. *The troubled crusade: American education 1945-1980*. New York: Basic Books.

Rehbein, J. 1984, *Diskurs und Versthen: Zur Role der Muttersprache bei der Textarbeitung in der Zweitsprache*. University of Hamburg.

Riel, M. 1983, The computer chronicles newswire: A functional learning environment for acquiring literacy skills. *Journal of Educaional Computing Research*, *1*, 317-337.

Rodriguez, R. 1982, *Hunger of memory: The education of Richard Rodriguez*. Boston: David R. Godine.

Rodriguez, R. 1985, Bilingualism, con: Outdated and unrealistic. *New York Times*, Education, Fall Survey, Sunday, November 10, Section 12, p. 83.

Rosier, P. & Holm, W. 1980, *The Rock Point experience: A longitudinal study of a Navajo school program*. Washington, D.C.: Center for Applied Linguistics.

Rosa, A. & Moll, L.C. 1985, Computadores, comunicacion y educacion: una colaboracion internacional en la intervencion e investigacion educativa. *Infancia y Aprendizaje, 30,* 1-17.

Rueda, R. & Mercer, J.R.   1985, Predictive analysis of decision-making with language minority handicapped children.   Paper presented at the BUENO Center 3rd Annual Symposium on Bilingual Education, Denver.

Rushdie, S. 1987, *The jaguar smile: A Nicaraguan journey.*   London: Picador.

Ryan, W. 1972, *Blaming the victim.*   New York: Vintage.

Sanchez, G. 1943, Pachucos in the making. *Common Ground, 4,* 13 - 20.

Santiago, R.L.   1985, Understanding bilingual education - or the sheep in wolf's clothing. *Educational Leadership,* September, 79-83.

Sayers, D. 1986a, From journal to journalism: ESL writers. *Puerto Rico TESOL-Gram, 13,* 7-8.

Sayers, D. 1986b, Sending messages across the classroom and around the world.   *Computer-Assisted Language Learning.   Special Supplement No. 3 of TESOL Newsletter, 20,* 7-8.

Sayers, D. 1988, "We are no longer alone:" Sixty-four years of sister classes in Celestin Freinet's Modern School Movement. *Bilingual Literacy Correspondent, 5,* 2-3.

Sayers, D. & Brown, K. 1987, Bilingual education and telecommunications: A perfect fit. *The Computing Teacher, 17,* 23-24.

Schlossman, S. 1983, Self-evident remedy?   George I Sanchez, Segregation, and Enduring Dilemmas in Bilingual Education. *Teachers College Record, 84,* 871-907.

Shanker, A. 1987, Reforms need close look. *Education Week,* January 14, p. 13.

Shor, I. 1987, *Critical teaching and everyday life.*   Chicago: University of Chicago Press.

Skutnabb-Kangas, T. 1984, *Bilingualism or not: The education of minorities.*   Clevedon, England: Multilingual Matters.

Skutnabb-Kangas, T. 1985, Resource power and autonomy through discourse in conflict: A Finnish migrant school strike in Sweden. In R. Phillipson & T. Skutnabb-Kangas, 1986, *Linguicism rules in education.* Doctoral dissertation submitted to Roskilde University, Denmark.

Skutnabb-Kangas, T. & Toukomaa, P. 1976, *Teaching migrant children's mother tongue and learning the language of the host country in the context of the sociocultural situation of the migrant family.* Helsinki: The Finnish National Commission for UNESCO.

Skutnabb-Kangas, T. & Cummins, J. in press, *Minority education: From shame to struggle.* Clevedon, England: Multilingual Matters.

Slavin, R.E. 1983, When does cooperative learning increase student achievement? *Psychological Bulletin, 94,*429-445.

Smith, F. 1978, *Understanding reading. 2nd edition.* New York: Holt, Rinehart & Winston.

Smith, F. 1982, *Writing and the writer.* New York: Holt, Rinehart & Winston.

Smith, F. 1983, Afterthoughts. In F. Smith, *Essays into Literacy.* Exeter, Hew Hampshire: Heinemann Educational Books, Inc.

Snow, C. 1983, Literacy and language: Reslationships during the preschool years. *Harvard Educational Review, 53,* 165-189.

Snow, C., Cancino, H., Gonzalez, P. & Shriberg, E. 1987, *Second language learners' formal definitions: An oral language correlate of school literacy.* Los Angeles: Center for Language Education and Research.

Swain, M. 1979, Bilingual education: Research and its implications. In C.A. Yorio, K. Perkins & J. Schachter (Eds.) *On TESOL '79: The learner in focus.* Washington, D.C.: TESOL.

Swain, M. 1986, Communicative competence: Some roles of comprehensible input and comprehensible output in its development. In J. Cummins and M. Swain, *Bilingualism in education: Aspects of theory, research and practice.* London: Longman.

Swain, M. & Lapkin, S. 1982, *Evaluating bilingual education.* Clevedon, England: Multilingual Matters.

Swain, M. & Wong Fillmore, L.W. 1984, Child second language development: Views from the field on theory and research. Paper presented at the 18th Annual TESOL Conference,

Houston Texas, March.

Taba, H. 1965, The teaching of thinking. *Elementary English, 42,* 534-542.

Troike, R. 1978, Research evidence for the effectiveness of bilingual education. *NABE Journal, 3,* 13-24.

Tizard, J., Schofield, W.N. & Hewison, J. 1982, Collaboration between teachers and parents in assisting children's reading. *British Journal of Educational Psychology, 52,* 1-15.

Topping, K.J. 1986, *Parents as educators: Training parents to teach their children.* London: Croom Helm.

Topping, K.J. & Wolfendale, S. 1985, *Parental involvement in children's reading.* London: Croom Helm.

Treger, B. & Wong, B.K. 1984, The relationship between native and second language reading comprehension and second language oral ability. In C. Rivera (Ed.), *Placement procedures in bilingual education: Education and policy issues.* Clevedon, England: Multilingual Matters.

Troike, R. 1978, Research evidence for the effectiveness of bilingual education. *NABE Journal, 3,* 13-24.

Tschanz, L. 1980, *Native languages and government policy: An historical examination.* Native Language Research Series No. 2, Centre for Research and Teaching of Canadian Native Languages, The University of Western Ontario.

U.S. Commission on Civil Rights 1973, *Teachers and students: Differences in teacher interaction with Mexican-American and Anglo students.* Washington, D.C.: U.S. Government Printing Office.

United States v. State of Texas 1981, Civil action # 5281 (Bilingual Education) Memorandum Opinion, January 1981.

United States General Accounting Office, 1987, *Bilingual education: A new look at the research evidence.* Briefing report to the Chairman, Committee on Education and Labor, House of Representatives. Washington, D.C.: GAO.

Valdes-Fallis, G. 1978, *Code switching and the clssroom teacher.* Language in Education Series, No. 4, Arlington, VA: Center for Applied Linguistics.

Vildomec, V. 1963, *Multilingualism.* Leyden: A.W. Sythoff.

Wallerstein, N. 1983, The teaching approach of Paulo Freire. In J.W. Oller, Jr. and P.A. Richard-Amato (Eds.) *Methods that work: A smorgasbord of ideas for language teachers.* Rowley, Mass: Newbury House.

Wells, G. 1982, Language, learning and the curriculum. In G. Wells, *Language, learning and education.* Bristol: Centre for the Study of Language and Communication, University of Bristol.

Wells, G. 1986, *The meaning makers.* Portsmouth, NH: Heinemann.

Willig, A.C. 1981-82, The effectiveness of bilingual education: Review of a report. *NABE Journal, 6,* 1-19.

Willig, A.C. 1985, A meta-analysis of selected studies on the effectiveness of bilingual education. *Review of Educational Research, 55,* 269-317.

Wong Fillmore, L. 1983, The language learner as an individual: Implications of research on individual differences for the ESL teacher. In M.A. Clarke and J. Handscombe (Eds.) *On TESOL '82: Pacific perspectives on language learning and teaching.* Washington, DC: TESOL.

Wright, R. 1987, Escape to Canada. *Saturday Night,* May 1987, p. 44-52.

Membership Benefits

Join the **CABE** team. Through your membership dues and involvement, you have the opportunity to make integral contributions towards positive educational change for limited-English proficient students. Membership benefits include:

■ **CABE Newsletter** – a bi-monthly issue bringing you the most recent updates and developments in the theory and practice of bilingual education.

■ **Information Updates** – Members receive information on current legislative and policy developments related to the field of bilingual education.

■ **Professional Development** – CABE offers local and regional educational seminars and the opportuninty to network with other professionals in your field of interest.

■ **Discounts** – Discounts on the annual statewide conference and **CABE** publications and materials.

■ **CABE Membership Reception** – CABE honors its members at its annual statewide conferences.

■ **Chapter Involvement** – CABE members may choose to involve themselves in the activities of local chapters and/or statewide affiliates.

CABE members may join a chapter and/or statewide affiliate, which will receive 20% of your dues. Please ☑ your selection below:

REGION I CHAPTERS
(03) Bay Area (BACA)
(15) Greater Santa Cruz Area
(49) North Valley (Chico)
(45) Richmond (RABE)
(07) Sacramento (SALSA)
(23) San Francisco (SFABE)
(11) San José Pueblo
(17) Truckee
(13) U.O.P./Delta Area
(28) Vintage (Napa, Sonoma)

REGION II CHAPTERS
(02) Bakersfield (BABE)
(41) Fresno
(33) Madera
(31) Salinas (SABE)
(37) South San Joaquin Valley
(12) Stanislaus County

REGION III CHAPTERS
(47) ABC
(01) Alhambra
(46) Azusa/Canyon City
(16) Compton
(38) El Monte
(14) L.A./U.S.C.
        (cont'd)

REGION III (cont'd)
(32) Lawndale
(27) Lynwood
(04) Montebello
(26) North Orange County (La Habra)
(25) Northridge (SUBE)
(05) Orange County
(39) Paramount
(40) Pasadena
(24) Pomona
(08) Santa Barbara
(42) Santa Paula
(21) South East Los Angeles (SELA)
(18) Southern Counties Administrators
(20) Ventura County
(48) Ventura/Oxnard (VOC)
(34) Whittier

REGION IV CHAPTERS
(43) Chino
(36) Coachella Valley
(35) Hemet/San Jacinto
(44) Imperial Valley
(29) North San Diego
(30) Redlands
(06) Riverside
(10) San Diego

STATEWIDE AFFILIATE
(19) California Association for Secondary Bilingual Education(CASBE)

( ) Other _____ (99) Member-at-large

CABE now accepts dues through payroll deduction with participating school districts. For information on how your district can participate, please contact your Chapter President or CABE Headquarters.

MEMBERSHIP APPLICATION

Please make check payable to CABE and mail with this completed form to:

CABE Headquarters • 926 J Street, Suite 810 • Sacramento, CA 95814 • (916) 447-3986

PLEASE TYPE OR PRINT CLEARLY as your future mailings depend on this application. ☐NEW ☐RENEWAL ☐LAPSED (over 1 year) ☐ADDRESS or NAME CHANGE

NAME: LAST _____ FIRST _____ PHONE #W:( ) _____ H:( ) _____

ADDRESS: _____ CITY: _____ STATE: _____ ZIP: _____

CABE members may join a local chapter and/or statewide affiliate, which receive 20% of your dues: (See list on reverse.)
[F1] Chapter _____ and/or Affiliate _____
( ) Please send information on how to start a **CABE** Chapter in my area. [F2]( ) Do not wish my name to be given out for mailing list purposes.

CABE Dues

[F5] ☐ $45 Administrator(0027) ☐ $35 Teacher(0021) ☐ $15 Paraprofessional(0022) ☐ $15 Student(0024) ☐ $15 Parent/Community(0023) ☐ $150 Institution/Organization/Commercial(0026)
[F7] Area of Interest: ☐ Preschool(PS) ☐ Elementary(ELEM) ☐ Secondary(SEC) ☐ Adult Ed. (ADED) ☐ College(COL) ☐ Teacher Training(TRNG)

Payroll Deduction

If your school district has payroll deduction for CABE dues, please attach, in lieu of a check, your completed payroll deduction form as required by your district. If you need information on how to start payroll deduction for CABE dues in your district, please check here. ( ) [F9] [P/R]

Contribution

☐ I would like to contribute to **CABE's** continuing efforts to strengthen Bilingual Education in California with my tax-deductible contribution of:

☐ $25 ☐ $50 ☐ $100 ☐ Other $ _____

PLEASE MARK YOUR CHAPTER AND AFFILIATE CHOICES ON REVERSE.

OFC USE	CK/PO#:	DATE RCVD:	ENTD:	MBR CRD:	[F3] EXP DATE:	[F6] REG:	COMP #:

New Monograph Shows

BILINGUAL EDUCATION WORKS!

On Course: Bilingual Education's Success in California by Drs. Stephen Krashen and Douglas Biber dispels some of the most commonly held myths about bilingual education. Building on a description of the principles underlying successful programs for limited English proficient children, the authors explore..."how language is acquired, how literacy is developed and how the proper use of the child's first language can accelerate both of these processes."

Programs consistent with sound principles of bilingual education are examined and through a review of data from operating California bilingual programs, the authors establish that students in properly designed programs..."acquire English rapidly and achieve good scores on academic tests whether tested in English or their first language."

In a remarkably lucid analysis Krashen and Biber demonstrate that bilingual programs which are well implemented and theoretically sound have strong positive effects on student academic achievement. This book should be compulsory, back to basics reading for all those who oppose bilingual education.
Dr. Jim Cummins
Associate Professor
Ontario Institute for
Studies in Education

An outstanding piece of work. Krashen and Biber convincingly show that bilingual education is the solution, not the problem.
Dr. Fred Tempes
Assistant Superintendent
Instructional Support
Service Division
California State Department
of Education

" . . . Educators who empower minority students by promoting their linguistic talents are also empowering their nation . . . "
—*from the Foreword*

EMPOWERING MINORITY STUDENTS

By Jim Cummins

"In a fundamental sense, educators who empower minority students by promoting their linguistic talents are also empowering their nation, and to a much greater extent than those who have committed themselves to squandering its human resources."

Empowering Minority Students proposes a framework for understanding why certain minority groups tend to experience persistent school failure and how this pattern of school failure can be reversed. The framework attempts to distill the essential features of programs that have successfully promoted minority students' academic growth and the characteristics of educators who have made these programs work. Almost invariably, programs that succeed in promoting minority students' academic growth develop in students a strong sense of confidence in who they are and in their ability to learn. They empower students. The educators who have initiated and taught in these programs have had the personal confidence and courage to defend them against reactions ranging from skepticism to overt racism.

Among the chapters included are:

- Historical and Political Context
- The Two Faces of Language Proficiency
- Double-Talk and Double-Think: Bilingualism and Children's Development in School
- Towards Anti-Racist Education: Empowering Minority Students
- Implementing Change: Challenging the Disabling Structure
- Disinformation in the Information Age: The Academic Critics of Bilingual Education
- "Against American Concepts": Bilingual Education—Subversive or Patriotic?
